D1565385

THE PEASANT SOUL OF JAPAN

The Peasant Soul of Japan

Shoichi Watanabe

Professor of English Studies
Sophia University, Tokyo

Foreword by Louis Allen

St. Martins' Press   New York

First published in the United States of America in 1989

Printed in Hong Kong

ISBN 0–312–03236–6

Library of Congress Cataloging-in-Publication Data

Watanabe, Shoichi, 1930–
[Nihon soshite nihonjin. English:
The peasant soul of Japan/Shoichi Watanabe; foreword by Louis Allen.
p. cm.
Translation of: Nihon soshite nihonjin.
Includes index.
ISBN 0–312–03236–6
1. National characteristics, Japanese. I. Title.
DS830.W32813 1989
952.04–dc20   89–6289
                                                          CIP

Contents

List of Maps

Foreword

Shoichi Watanabe is a Professor of English at Sophia University, one of the most renowned private universities in Tokyo. A knowledgeable historian of English-language studies, a bibliophile whose collection of English first editions would be the envy of many a book collector, he is also the author of a best-selling book on the German General Staff, a disciple of forgotten Victorian figures like Samuel Smiles and P. G. Hamerton, the father of a gifted musical family, and a Roman Catholic.

In short, Watanabe is a very diverse and quirky Japanese, who is also passionately interested in the foibles of his own people and in their history. This has led him to contribute to the many theories of Japanese identity which have become a flourishing brand of Japanese speculative historical and psychological writing since 1945.

This book is his chief contribution to that debate. It draws on Japanese and European classical literature, on the history of warfare, on studies of law and business management. It is opinionated, and at times both infuriating and fascinating. The reader will feel an urge to argue with Watanabe in profound disagreement; he or she will also come across sudden insights which illuminate Japanese behaviour arising from the most trivial domestic arrangements, for instance, the nomenclature of the Japanese lavatory; or from the most far-reaching events, such as the outbreak of the war in the Pacific.

As a television personality and a commentator on current affairs in Japan's leading periodicals, Professor Watanabe is an influential and controversial figure in modern Japan. Whether we agree with him or not, we should be aware of what he thinks.

Louis Allen

Preface

JAPAN AS A COUNTRY OF DON PEASANTS

When did I first decide to write about my own people, the Japanese? I'm pretty sure I was in the mood to do it when I was a student in Europe, when I was 25. At that time, though, the urge to write about Europe was stronger.

The notion that I had to write, at all costs, came to me after I'd been to America, about two decades ago. I was extremely anxious that my American colleagues and students should understand what sort of a country Japan was, what kind of people the Japanese were. I also thought that my fellow countrymen might be interested in my theories.

That was why I published *The Japanese in the light of their history*,[1] which went through its 30th printing recently. That was the beginning of my commitment to theories about the Japanese. Two years later, in 1975, I came to grasp the essential features of the Japanese as those of a peasant, whom I call respectfully and humorously 'Don Peasant'. This happened while I was writing a thesis titled—*The Equestrian State and the Peasant State*—comparing the Americans and the Japanese.[2]

The Pacific War, or the Greater East Asia War as we, the Japanese, used to call it, remains an inexhaustible quarry of ideas and reflections for me. In the course of the war the characteristic features of two nations were revealed, it seems to me, at their most typical. Finally I was led to a dichotomy of national mentality—the equestrian mentality and the peasant mentality. This dichotomy of mine is far from flawless like most other dichotomies, and for that matter, like any classification in any other field, but it sheds a new light on the national propensity of the Japanese.

Throughout this book two concepts of the 'equestrian' and the 'peasant' mentality are used in a special sense. An 'equestrian' people need not necessarily live on horseback while a peasant nation does not necessarily live in rice paddies. These two concepts are derived from two contrasting ways of living, and seem to be applicable to different national mentalities long after a nation has ceased to live either on horseback or in rice paddies.

We can think of a village community in which the existence of each member depended on farming a small portion of land. As far as he was working, he could subsist somehow. His safety was, as it were, dependent on that small portion of land. His ability was not important. Everyone in that community worked on a small lot of land. They did not need to, or to be precise, were not allowed to compete with other members of their community. They could not, or were not allowed to, beat or destroy through competition any other member of their community. No single person was that much more efficient in farming than any other. The rice produced by one peasant tasted exactly as good as any other's. These peasants did not feel any particular need for an able leader and their leader was not selected or elected by criteria concerning ability, but by the standard of how old his family was, how old and how good-natured he was. Insofar as a member's family was one of the oldest in that community, insofar as he was one of the oldest among his equals, insofar as he was good-natured enough and rich enough to spare some of his time and means to help other community members, his qualifications for becoming head of the community were enough. More exactly or ironically speaking, the more evidently incompetent and lacking in ability he was, the more popular he tended to be among his fellow villagers. Even if he was incapacitated with palsy, he could be a popular village headman. The existence of the villagers had been safe since time immemorial except for those occasions when natural calamities such as typhoons and earthquakes took place, and then everybody knew that these natural calamities were beyond the control of all human abilities and efforts. With a good-natured, generous, inarticulate old man of an old family as their headman, the villagers felt satisfied realising that such an old man was not their chief by virture of his ability or effectiveness. They felt relieved to know that no element of competition was included there. To be able to feel satisfaction in this way was what was most important. The village was safe regardless of the personal abilities of its headman.

To feel relaxed and free from competition among the members of a community—this is the essence of what is called Japanese 'wa' (harmony). If this kind of existence is placed at one extreme end of the typology of cultures, we could place the existence of 'mounted bandits' at the other equally extreme end. While peasants locate the basis of their safety in the farming soil, 'mounted bandits' find theirs in something quite different. They must keep moving and keep fighting, with the result that their safety depends greatly on the capability and effectiveness of their leader. An inarticulate senile old man could never be entrusted with the leadership of the band, however good-natured he may be. Ability, effectiveness, competition, leadership are the most important values among mounted bandits. A society in which these values are of dominant importance is called in my terminology 'equestrian', while a society in which the values of peasant villagers are preponderant is called in my terminology 'peasant' or 'agararian'.

If I refer to the Japanese generals during the Pacific War as 'peasants' this does not mean that they come from peasant families (although this was sometimes the case), but that their way of thinking is visibly coloured by peasant values. They took it for granted that Japan was safe forever in the same way that the peasants took it for granted that they could place their safety in their plots of land. The quality of leadership was markedly different from that of the American Army in which those qualities which I call 'equestrian' were more dominant.

I have read numerous books on the Japanese written by Japanese and non-Japanese, and have found so far no contradiction between their conclusions and mine. The original Japanese version of this book was published eight years ago and is now in its 19th printing. This infers that my analysis of the Japanese has been accepted by a very wide range of my fellow countrymen. In the course of these eight years I have been asked by a great variety of groups—some consisting of career government officials, and others of entrepreneurs and executives—to talk about the characteristic features of the Japanese. All of my audience—I can hardly think of any exception—have given a nodding acceptance to my theory. This seems to show that my view of the Japanese people has been regarded by responsible leaders of various sects in Japan as an analysis which explains very well the innermost motives felt by them. With this remark it is not meant that the Japanese race is an exclusive, pure crystalline sample of this ethnological type. The same features may be shared in various degrees by other nations. It remains, however, quite true that a great number of Japanese in responsible posts do feel themselves as analysed in the following chapters. I hope this small book will help other peoples to understand what the Japanese are, or at least what they think themselves to be.

NOTES

1. Nihonshi kara mita Nihonjin, 2 vols. (Sanno University Press, 1973).
2. This was for *The Shokun*, a monthly opinion moulder (Bungei-shunju, November 1975).

Simplified Chronology of Japanese History

538	The Buddhist sutras reach Japan.
622	Prince Shōtoku dies.
710	Nara becomes the Capital City.
794	Kyoto becomes the Capital City. The start of the Heian Period.
850	About this time the Fujiwara Clan becomes dominant.
1166	The Heike (= Taira Clan) become dominant. This clan is a Buke (warrior clan).
1192	The Genji (= Minamoto Clan) become dominant. This clan is a Buke (warrior clan).
1334	The Kenmu Restoration (fought for by Masashige Kusunoki).
1336	The Ashikaga Clan (warrior clan) becomes dominant.
1392	The Ashikaga Shogunate or Muromachi Period begins.
1467	Ōnin Disturbance. The start of the Great Civil War, that is, the Sengoku Period (War Period) which lasts until 1603, when the Tokugawa Shogunate starts.
1560	Nobunaga ODA becomes dominant.
1573	The Ashikaga Shogunate comes to an end.
1590	Hideyoshi TOYOTOMI dominates the whole nation.
1600	Battle of Sekigahara.
1603	Ieyasu TOKUGAWA founds the shogunate in Edo (= Tokyo) and Edo becomes the centre of administration, while Kyoto remains the Capital City. The Tokugawa Period (= Edo Period) begins.
1868	Meiji Restoration. Emperor Meiji comes to Edo and renames it Tokyo. Feudalism comes to an end, marking the beginning of modern Japan.
1877	Takamori Saigo rises against the central government and is soon crushed.
1894–95	Sino-Japanese War (in which Japan is victorious).
1904–05	Russo-Japanese War (in which Japan is victorious).
1908–41	Anti-Japanese sentiment and violence grows in the US.
1932	Manchukuo, the new state of Manchu, is founded.
1937	The Sino-Japanese Incident breaks out.
1941	The Pacific War breaks out.
1945	The surrender of Japan.

Part I
Prologue

1 The Tokyo Summit of 1979: An event which sheds light on the nature of the Japanese

In the summer of 1979, although it was the hot season in Tokyo, the streets were crowded with police wearing thick uniforms and helmets. It was the opening of the Tokyo Economic Summit conference. Although we are an old country—it has been said that it is about 2650 years since the nation was founded—prime ministers of other countries had never assembled in Japan before. The Summit could almost be called the greatest ceremony since the founding of the state.

The focus of debate was the problem of energy. It was clear to most people that the oil crisis was the big question dominating world events. As Japan is very short of oil supplies, and yet had weathered the oil crisis splendidly, it was deeply significant that the 1979 Summit, otherwise known as 'The Oil Summit', should open in Tokyo.

A great deal of discussion on oil took place, but because the officials must have prepared the talks to a certain degree before the prime ministers' discussions, no particularly extraordinary conclusions were anticipated.

Although debates may have been fierce behind closed doors, the joint statement issued after the conference seemed to represent a unanimous verdict. It was observed, however, that there was another common topic among the prime ministers apart from oil which was the formal subject of the conference. This topic had apparently been argued about in informal gatherings. The Japanese prime minister, however, had taken no part in it, the other prime ministers had reached no harmony of views, and no joint statement had been issued. What then was this topic so eagerly debated by all the prime ministers behind the

3

scenes, in addition to the overt topic of the Tokyo Summit?
It was this:

'Why isn't Fukuda here?'

Prime Minister Fukuda had invited the Summit to meet
in Tokyo. But when the invited guests turned up in Tokyo
the following year, Fukuda did not put in an appearance
and they were met by a completely different Prime Minister.
What conclusions would have been drawn if this had
happened in Europe or America?

By and large, only six questions would have been put:

(1) Has Fukuda died of some disease, or been assassin-
    ated?
(2) Has he fallen seriously ill?
(3) Has a revolution broken out?
(4) Has he been defeated in a general election?
(5) Has some terrible government scandal been exposed,
    or has a severe economic crisis arisen, and a motion
    of No Confidence in the Cabinet been passed?
(6) Has he resigned?

In other countries, whether communist or democratic,
these would be the causes of a switch of political power.
Yet Prime Minister Fukuda's withdrawal was the result of
none of these things. It was as a result of a congress of the
ruling party that the party had fitted itself out with a new
head. Of course, in Europe and the United States, changes
of presidents do occur in party congresses of the ruling
party, but only when some policy has clearly failed or the
party has been defeated in a general election or when the
president has become seriously ill. Yet Japan's economy
was flourishing and running smoothly in an unprecedented
way. The crime rate was low, public order was properly
maintained, and Mr Fukuda was in good health. Yet, hard
as it must have been to those prime ministers gathered for
the Tokyo Summit to conceive, in Japan the change of
prime minister was natural. They must have thought Japan
an odd sort of country, and indeed it cannot have been
easy to understand in terms of practical politics for those
used to European or American democracy.

IN PRAISE OF THE 'DON' OF DON PEASANT

However, to the Japanese, there was and is nothing incomprehensible about why Mr Ohira took over from Mr Fukuda. How could I explain this? It occurred to me that I should try to interpret it from the point of view of Japanese history and Japanese racial characteristics. This book is the result.

Any convincing way of explaining the emergence of the Ohira Cabinet must also apply to explanations of the emergence of later cabinets. If the explanation seems to be reasonable, it should offer a feasible hypothesis for 'a theory of the Japanese' or 'a method of reading the Japanese people'.

As mentioned, I first published the considerations I put forward here in the short essay in *Shokun* (November 1975) entitled *The Equestrian State and the Peasant State*.[1]

The ideas put forward can be summed up in the phrase, 'The Japanese are basically Don Peasants'. I use the term 'Don Peasant' as a nickname for farming people, and as both my parents were the children of 'Don Peasants' the term has a more than ordinary significance for me.

When I consider my own nature what seems to be deepest within me is something I would like to call 'the nature of the Don Peasant'. This characteristic seems to be most noticeable in my fellow Japanese: a principle of action at work inside us. I thought I would like to link up the 'DON' of 'Don Peasant', which expresses both feelings of familiarity and slight contempt, with the Don of Don Quixote or Don Camillo, or the Don which is used for the head of the Mafia. My 'Don Peasant', that is to say, takes on something of the feeling of 'Lord Peasant' or 'Don Farmer'—a word implying a feeling of close kinship, a linking in a special way to one's own blood combined with special self-depreciation and respect.

The Japanese 'Don Peasant' or 'Don Farmer' is a wily customer. He can be petty, but he can display the nobility of self-sacrifice. You can find in him the good and the bad of the Japanese. Every people has its merits and defects, or rather, any people's merits can suddenly become defects, and vice versa. If we consider the basic nature of the Don Peasant we can see that, in spite of his many defects, not only are the roots of Japanese democracy visible in him, but we can discern from him how life will be lived on this planet in the future. So, as a clue to reading the psychology and behaviour of the Japanese, I would like to propose a 'theory of the Japanese Don Peasant'.

'JAPANESENESS' OBSERVED BY A SWISS PRIEST

A learned Swiss priest arrived in Japan in 1952, when the ruins of wartime destruction still remained here and there, even in the centre of the capital city of Tokyo, which was moving along the road to post-war recovery. He was born in German-speaking Switzerland and studied classical Chinese literature in London under Arthur Waley, famous as the English translator of *The Tale of Genji* and various Nō plays. He acquired a knowledge of and fondness for the culture of ancient Japan.

When he first came to Japan, post-war Americanisation was flourishing everywhere and Japanese culture was submerged in a sea of Americanisation or Westernisation. He wondered in which sea it would sink. Many foreigners who knew Japan spoke in this way, deploring what was happening. Everywhere the liquidation of Japanese culture was apparent.

In general, the very notion of contemporary Japan, for Western minds, seems in itself to be a logical contradiction. They seem to think that whatever is contemporary is American or European, and not Japanese; moreover, that whatever is termed 'Japanese' cannot be contemporary. It was because the United States and European science and technology had influenced the Japanese indiscriminately that a country closed for a long time to the outside world became a great military nation which produced the Zero fighter and the battleship *Yamato* and, after being defeated in war, was rapidly becoming a great economic power. Foreigners were quite sure that this was because 'unJapanese things' were done. Foreigners who loved things Japanese were constantly dismayed and used to ask, 'Aren't you paying too high a price for the modernisation of Japan?'

Furthermore, when they enquired more deeply into things

Japanese, they were alarmed to discover that the modernisation of Japan was not merely a question of science and technology; the spiritual culture of the West had also penetrated deeply, to an unbelievable extent. For instance, when Hermann Hesse received the Nobel Prize in 1946, English and French critics were put to some inconvenience in finding out about this writer, who was almost totally untranslated in their countries. But a significant number of Japanese, even middle-school pupils, had read one or two books by him, since selections of Hesse had existed in Japanese in pre-war days.

This same Swiss priest spent his first year after coming to Japan in Iwate Prefecture at the northern tip of the Japanese mainland, ending up in a cold village in a region which is nicknamed the 'Japanese Tibet'. It was in this out-of-the-way spot that he was accosted by a man asking his advice on, of all things, the thoughts of Max Weber. When their experiences of this kind multiplied, most Americans or Europeans felt that Japan was rushing headlong into Westernisation and they lamented the disappearance of the old romantic Japan: Mount Fuji, cherry blossom, geisha. This Swiss priest was himself one of those old hands in understanding Japanese culture.

However, after he had stayed in Japan for some time, he observed, 'The Japanese have never changed: they are the same as they have always been'. The peasants of northeastern Japan handled the most recent fertilisers and farm machinery, but when they sowed their seed they waited for the traditional sign, a transformation of melting snow which must assume the shape of a horse; that is, they waited for news from the god of the mountain before they planted their seeds. The Hitachi Factory produces electronic equipment of the highest degree of sophistication, but in every factory is enshrined Kumano Gongen (the avatar of Mount Kumano), a residue of the old mountain myth probably connected to the local shrine whose priest performed the purification rite, or 'ground breaking', for the factory premises.

When the International Exhibition—Expo 70—was being set up, the organisers were afraid of the curse of the gods of the earth, and a female medium (miko) was brought in to dedicate a dance and pray for the safety of the buildings.

The Swiss priest noticed that everywhere in Japan old primitive notions co-existed alongside the most up-to-date technology, and finally, he came to certain conclusions using the metaphor of the crystal to explain it.

The Crystal which lies in the heart of hearts of the 'Don Peasant'

'Crystallography teaches us that every crystal contains a lattice structure model ... This determines the mode of incorporation when a substance is absorbed into the whole, but the model itself never reveals its own form.

In exactly the same way, there exists a crystal lattice in the heart of the Japanese, which is not evident to the eye, but which, when foreign substances are taken into the structure of Japanese culture, has apparently a decisive function in passing the substance through a subtle assimilative process until it is finally transformed into the substance of the Japanese themselves ...'

This Swiss priest is Thomas Immoos (now a professor at Sophia University and also of the Faculty of Letters of Tokyo University) who has written a book called *The Unchanging People*.[2]

Why does he think this? He continues,

Japanese of the present day, live in western-style flats, ride in automobiles, wear Western clothing, and have a taste for Western food. In spite of this, the value system which lies at the basis of the behaviour and feelings of the Japanese is peculiar to them. There exist no words in foreign languages which correspond to the core concepts of this system, ON, GIRI, NINJO, WABI, SABI.[3]

The ultra-radical student activists of today's Japan quote at length from Marx, Mao Tse-tung and Marcuse. But their organisation, their modes of conduct, their tactics, and their emotions are barely different from those of the *samurai* and *yakuza* (gangsters) of the Tokugawa period of the 17th Century. It follows that Western concepts are inadequate for the analysis of Japanese reality. Japan is different both from the national capitalism of communist countries and from the private capitalism of the West. It is a society quite unlike any other. Nothing like Japan Inc. has ever existed in the world before. For this very reason, Japan was a revelation to the million foreign visitors to the 1970 International Exhibition. Their eyes were opened to what Japan is like today, and what perhaps the world will be like tomorrow.[4]

Professor Immoos says that this 'crystal lattice' is not immediately obvious in the Japanese nature but that it does finally subsume into a Japanese form everything which comes in from outside. He points out, for instance, that what we term 'Marxism', a foreign substance, has become a Japanese-style movement as a result of this process.

At a superficial glance, the Japanese appear to be 'foreignising' themselves. If, however, you peel off the top layer of skin, the spiritual structure which reveals itself can only be Japanese. Professor Immoos first recognised the crystal structure which is for him the spiritual structure of the Japanese in the value system of the concepts ON, GIRI, NINJO, WABI, SABI. I agree with him in that even though the Japanese appear to be changing a great deal, they are at heart an 'unchanging people'.

At the core of this, in my view, lies the mentality of the 'Don Peasant'. Concepts such as GIRI and NINJO which are considered to be a peculiarly Japanese value system should be considered, as I see it, as arising from this 'Don Peasant' mentality. So we must ask ourselves, what is the nature of the peasant mentality?

To define in a particular phrase what we mean by the 'nature of the peasant' we should probably term it 'the way of life peculiar to an agrarian society'.

To clarify the method of defining this agricultural society, let us compare and contrast the characteristics of a pastoral society and an equestrian nomad society, which might be regarded as its extreme opposite. Of course, what we term the mentality of an agrarian society and that of an equestrian society does not exist in a completely pure form at all; but there is certainly a type of society we can call 'agrarian' and one we can call 'equestrian'. Let us compare them from several points of view, from which it will then be clear at a glance into which category we should place Japanese society.

First of all consider the way of thinking about 'the land'. Peasants cling closely to the land as a matter of course. As the productivity of the land, particularly of the rice paddy, is very high, even a small area takes on great significance. In the past, if there was a difference of two inches in the boundary line between two neighbouring fields, or a falsification of the boundary by three inches, a conflict would ensue which might last for two or three generations.

The way of thinking from which derives the term ISSHOKENMEI is a development of this concept. When we do something eagerly and with enthusiasm, we say we are doing it *isshokenmei* (literally 'with the zeal of one *place*' or, 'as eagerly as if one's whole life depended on one place'). As Japanese samurai were originally of the landowning class, they were very sensitive about land.

From about the end of the period of the Ancient Laws which marked the beginning of the Kamakura period (second half of the 12th century), the word *isshokenmei* became current; it arose from the notion of protecting the life (kenmei) of the clan in one place (issho) at a time of conflict and litigation, since the basis of life for the samurai lay in one not very extensive fief.[5]

The idea of *Kenmei* ('with the zeal of life') and *inochi-gake* ('at the risk of one's life') persists to this day where the land is concerned. Even people who live in Tokyo care desperately about land because their parents or grandparents were peasants. For example, it is the general rule to build a fence in collaboration with one's neighbour occupying equal space either side of the exact boundary between two houses. If the thickness of the fence or wall is four inches, two inches fall either side of the line. What happens, though, if one of the parties says, 'This house doesn't need a fence'? Or if there is nobody living next door? When that happens, the man who wants the fence has it put up, four inches wide, inside his own property. He loses two inches of boundary-land as well as what it will cost him to build the fence, compared with what it would have cost if he had shared it with his neighbour. It will be a cause of deep resentment to him that he has had to build entirely inside his own property and has lost a boundary space of two inches, and it is not unusual to come across people who have lived for decades loathing their next-door neighbours as a result.

'LAND-NEUROSIS'

Of course, there is an attachment to the earth in human beings who belong to an equestrian society, too, but the nature of the attachment is different. Let us, for instance, consider the life of nomads. How many families can live on a grassy plain about the size of Tokyo? The answer is only five or six.

The notion of a conflict over one or two inches of boundary between neighbouring houses is ridiculous to those whose sheep on pasture must be continuously on the move. Equally, the space occupied by a clan pasturing its flocks is of an extent inconceivable to a farmer with his rice paddy field, and is fundamentally different from the attachment to the land of an agrarian people.

We can observe two forms of spirit arising from this: the spirit which displays a closeness to the earth itself, and the spirit which gladly moves over land. If war breaks out, these two spirits show a marked contrast in reaction.

NOTES

1. This thesis is included in my book *The Age of Justice* (Bungei Shunju, 1977).
2. *Kawarazaru minzoku* (Nansosha, 1972).
3. These terms are in constant use in Japanese social sciences, history and art criticism. They might be roughly rendered as follows:
    on—a debt of gratitude, such as children owe to their parents;
    giri—obligation, sense of duty, giving rise to rigid social customs;
    ninjo—sympathy, humanity, compassion such as one naturally feels towards others, as with parents or lovers;
    sabi—elegant simplicity;
    wabi—quiet refinement.
    D. Suzuki, in *Zen and Japanese Culture* (pp. 23–4) gives the following definitions:

'*Sabi* consists in rustic unpretentiousness or archaic imperfection, apparent simplicity or effortlessness in execution, and richness in historical associations; 'to be poor, that is, not to be dependent on things worldly—wealth, power and reputation—and yet to feel inwardly the presence of something of the highest value, above time and social position: this is what essentially constitutes *wabi*'.

4.   Immoos, op. cit., p. 25.
5.   The Kamakura period saw the transfer of power from the civilian to the military firmly established when the Minamoto clan finally unseated the Taira clan and established a new government away from Kyoto in Kamakura. A new military aristocracy, descending from sons of nobles, former district governors and managers of family estates, was born, headed by the Shogun's vassals or retainers, the so-called Kenin, whose privileged economic status was assured by official recognition of their fiefs. Below the Kenin were the Samurai, who were also mounted warriors commanding their own sub-vassals, although they were initially known as persons who waited on or attended to someone else.

2 The Peasant Spirit in War: The Agrarian and Equestrian Mentalities

A 'GREAT GENERAL'

Although both Japan and China are agrarian societies, in the course of their history their representative great generals have had the peculiar characteristic of showing little attachment to the land. As great generals of Japan and China we might select Kusunoki Masashige (d. 1336) and Chu Kê K'ung Ming (d. 234) respectively. In the case of Kusunoki Masashige,[1] from the time he first stood up against the Kamakura shogunate he seems to have considered withdrawing from the battlefield. Masashige raised his flag in Akasaka Castle and harried the shogun's army by his skilful tactics, yet he does not appear to have thought it vital to hold on to this little castle for ever, or to carry out some glorious deed such as dying in battle, or defending the castle to the last. He hid for a while, then recaptured the castle. The shogun then raised a huge army and attacked Akasaka Castle, whereupon Masashige abandoned it and withdrew ten kilometres farther into the interior to Chihaya Castle in the most mountainous region, which the forces of the shogunate failed to reduce. In the meanwhile, other forces hostile to the shogun arose and his armies were finally overthrown.

The so-called Kemmu Restoration,[2] 1334, which began in this way, did not last long. Ashikaga Takauji, the founder of the Ashikaga shogunate (1338–1573) rebelled against the Imperial Court and led a large army from Chinzei (Kyūshū) against Kyoto. Masashige proposed a basic strategy to the Imperial Court: the Imperial Army was inferior in numbers and could not prevail over Takauji's army in a frontal attack, so the Emperor should flee to Mount Hiei, near Kyoto, which would mean that Kyoto would be occupied by the

Ashikaga forces. Masashige's army would then begin to move from its base at Kawachi (see Map 1, p. 187) and cut communications between Kyoto and the Inland Sea. The Ashikaga army's supplies came from the Inland Sea, and if that route were cut, the larger the army in Kyoto, the more acute would become the problem of food supplies. Since the Ashikaga army merely consisted of clans each seeking its own self-interest, if the Emperor hoisted aloft the imperial brocade banner and attacked, he would certainly be victorious. Such was Kusunoki Masashige's strategy. It involved abandoning Kyoto, which was undoubtedly the most important piece of territory in the whole of Japan. But his prime objective was to win the war and he viewed with equanimity the tactical, short-term disposal of territory.

The men of the Imperial Court on the other hand clung to the notion of territory. The refusal to abandon land was stronger in them than the desire for the ultimate objective, victory. So Kusunoki Masashige's plan was rejected. He was, in effect, defeated politically by the power of the peasant mentality of the Imperial Court. Washing his hands of them he rode out to Minatogawa (see Map 1, p. 187) to certain defeat and his forces were annihilated. He took his own life, as did his brother, Masasue, who vowed that he would be born again, seven times so that he might destroy the Emperor's armies; Masashige wholeheartedly agreed with this and left to posterity the slogan *shichisho hokoku*—'serve your country through seven lives'.

The *kamikaze* units of modern times who went out to battle and died in full knowledge that their cause was hopeless called themselves 'kikusui units' (kikusui or chrysanthemum water being the Kusunoki family emblem) and showed their sympathy with the spirit of Kusunoki Masashige by wearing forehead bands on which was written the phrase 'serve your country through seven lives'. More recently Mishima Yukio, the famous novelist, linked himself with this tradition when he committed suicide by cutting his belly open while wearing such a forehead band.

The basis of Kusunoki-style strategy is to consider only final victory, not to be dragged into retention of territory, and to revere Kusunoki Masashige as a great strategist means abandoning the spirit of attachment to the earth, which is the basic peasant's nature; in this respect his ideas were remote from the Japanese way of thinking.

THE EQUESTRIAN PHILOSOPHY OF WAR

The same can be said of Chu Kê K'ung Ming in the Chronicle of the Three Kingdoms (*c.* 290 AD). The direct way to victory of Liu Pei[3] came after the emergence of Tan Fy, who recommended K'ung Ming as strategic adviser. K'ung Ming's strategy also lay in abandoning the battlefield of inevitable defeat. The ancient Chinese were peasants, and when they controlled the battlefield they were concerned about seizing territory. After they had won on the field of battle they relaxed, whereupon K'ung Ming's army appeared from behind them, unscathed, and smashed them to smithereens—at least so the story goes. The special characteristics of K'ung Ming seem to consist of not clinging to territory in battle, of being able to retreat with an easy conscience, or to carry out a camouflaged retreat.

This style of fighting was quite central to the Chinese tradition which is why those generals who have used it have always stood out in history. But to a nomadic, equestrian society it comes as a natural tactic of warfare. Just consider the army of the archetypal nomadic people, the Mongols, a typical equestrian people, as described in the *Travels of Marco Polo*:

When these Tartars come to engage in battle, they never mix with the enemy, but keep hovering about him, discharging their arrows first from one side and then from the other, occasionally pretending to flee, and *during their flight shooting arrows backwards at their pursuers, killing men and horses, as if they were combating face to face.* In this sort of warfare, the adversary imagines he has gained a victory, when in fact he has lost the battle; for the Tartars, observing the mischief they have done him, wheel about, and renewing the fight, overpower his remaining troops, and make them prisoners in spite of their utmost exer-

tions. Their horses are so well broken-in to quick changes
of movement, that upon the signal given, they instantly
turn in every direction; and by these rapid manoeuvres
many victories have been obtained.[4]

I would like you to notice the phrases I have emphasised
in the quotation. It is quite clear from them that whether
the Mongol Army advances or retreats, there is no change
in its war-like spirit. That shows perfectly how an equestrian
society fights.

What finally matters in a battle is to win. Since little value
is placed on territory, there is no shame involved in retreat.
In the case of an agrarian people retreat implies withdrawal
from the land, the thing next in importance to life, or even
more important than life itself. The land which is held is
land held by struggling in one place (*isshokenmei*) and must
be preserved even at the cost of one's life. It is shameful to
lose it, and losing it constitutes defeat.

For nomadic people there is no such thing as land being
held by struggling in one place, so there is no great difference between the value of advance and the value of retreat.
It is shameful to stick to the battlefield where there is no
victory, and to make war where there are great casualties.
To leave a battlefield without wounds, or only slightly
damaged, is not to withdraw in defeat, but simply to retreat
tout court, to withdraw.

In nomadic society retreat implies neither defeat nor
shame. When Genghis Khan attacked in the West, he had
two of his generals, Bara and Toltai, pursue the son of the
Islamic Emperor Jalal-ud-Din and surround his force at
Multan. It was, at that time, in that city (which is now in
Pakistan) fearfully hot. The troops were tired out and their
horses exhausted. Epidemics broke out. Thereupon, both
generals halted at the opportune moment, called off their
attack on the city and withdrew. In the usual sense of the
word they had been repulsed, as the word is understood in
an agrarian society. But for the Mongol Army, based on an
equestrian society, there was no feeling of having been
defeated, even when they were forced to withdraw halfway
through their attack. They had sustained no great casualties
either to men or horses, and they were still buoyant and

triumphant. Those retreating armies laid waste Lahore, Peshawar and Malikpur; and still exulting in their victorious destiny, they rejoined the main forces of Genghis Khan.

Those towns which you failed to conquer in the hot season, you must attack again when it becomes a little cooler, spurring on your now well-fed horses. That is the nature of an equestrian people, a way of thinking you do not find among agrarian peoples. The warriors of an agrarian people who adapted this method in war were always revered for their originality.

Even in the case of the famous generals of the Civil War period (1467–1568)[5] in Japan, skill in battle has been equated with skilfully manipulating a retreat. Toyotomi Hideyoshi (d. 1598), a brilliant strategist and shrewd politician,[6] suffered a strategic setback at the hands of Tokugawa Ieyasu (d. 1616).[7] Hideyoshi promptly withdrew, although his main force was not defeated. Tokugawa Ieyasu was tactically victorious but he had no strength left with which to pursue Hideyoshi. He was finally coaxed into taking the oath of allegiance to Hideyoshi, who thus became the first unifier of a divided Japan.

Of course, we have to take the stories about Masashige, K'ung Ming and Hideyoshi with a pinch of salt, because they are stories rather than history, but if we consider them merely as showing a pattern of combat, we can see that the pattern they employed was not that of peasant thinking.

EQUESTRIAN AND AGRARIAN TACTICS IN THE PACIFIC WAR

National characteristics appear very clearly in time of war. The type of soldier who went out to fight in the last war was formed by his peace-time environment, and it is interesting to examine the differences in behaviour patterns displayed by the American and Japanese armies in the light of attachment to the land.

Although early settlers in North America were descendants of the European peasantry, they were forced to adopt new ways of thinking that were closer to those of an equestrian people. There are many tendencies in the strategic thinking of the US Army in which this is reflected.

When the Japanese hurled their forces against the Philippines, General MacArthur turned the Battaan Peninsula and the fortress of Corregidor (see Map 3, p. 189) into a base which held up the Japanese for three months. But he could not stop them completely, and, with the valedictory phrase 'I shall return', he made his escape by sea and air to Australia, across waters dominated by the air supremacy of the Japanese. This was on 17 March 1942.

Because he left his subordinates behind in the fortress of Corregidor, the Japanese at that time saw him as an irresponsible, even cowardly commander. We thought the supreme commander had deserted the battlefield. If it had been a Japanese general, as we saw it, he would have defended Corregidor with his men to the death and not left them behind in peril while he himself escaped to safety. This allowed us to indulge in a feeling of superiority.

It struck us as strange that MacArthur should afterwards be appointed Supreme Commander of the Allied forces in the south-west Pacific, without receiving the slightest punishment for what he did, though he scuttled away in an undignified manner and left his men to face the music.

It occurred to us, briefly, that perhaps the difference between American and Japanese generals was not a difference between inferior and superior but perhaps one between ways of thinking. But as the Japanese continued to win victory after victory, we took this to be proof of quality. Obviously, we thought, the Japanese way was superior to the American way.

Yet MacArthur was no defeated general fleeing the battlefield and losing his warlike spirit. The case was exactly like that of the general of the Mongol Army who fought on and maintained 'There is no shame in retreat . . . you can be as brave when you retreat as in the moment you start your attack.' In the event, MacArthur counterattacked boldly and courageously and his men's morale continued to rise.

From that point of view, the relation between the US task forces, which counterattacked by island-hopping across the Pacific, and the Japanese garrison units, can be compared with the relation between the cavalry units of Genghis Khan and the cities scattered in the oases. The American forces attacked by selecting significant spots from the strategic point of view: first Guadalcanal, then the Gilberts, Kwajalein, the Marianas, Iwojima and Okinawa (see Map 3, p. 189). They did not foolishly attempt to carry by storm places like Rabaul (Map 3), where stubborn resistance might be expected and casualties were likely to be high. Instead, they occupied a small island slightly to the north. Is this not in some respects similar to the encirclement of Multan by Genghis's chieftains, Bara and Toltai?

MACARTHUR AND THE PHILIPPINES

The mistake MacArthur made was the operation to retake the Philippines. In the judgement of the US Chiefs of Staff, it was unnecessary to recapture the Philippines. Once Saipan, Okinawa and Iwojima had fallen, there were enough springboards available for an offensive against the Japanese mainland: they therefore believed there was no point in retaking the Philippines by a landing operation. From the standpoint of the American Army, which was not a stickler for territory, this made sense. But out of deference to MacArthur's 'I shall return', the decision was taken to recapture the Philippines by force of arms, whatever the cost. Since MacArthur's prestige as the man who had retrieved the situation in the Pacific was enormous, all he had to do was express a wish, and the Combined Chiefs of Staff, grudgingly, authorised the operation.

With the advantage of hindsight, MacArthur's mistake is obvious even to the untutored eye. If there had been no Philippines operation, Japan would without doubt have been defeated anyway and the end of the war might have come much sooner. Manila would not have been turned into a battlefield, the casualties to the Filipinos would have been few, and furthermore the deaths and casualties suffered by so many Japanese and American soldiers would have been avoided. MacArthur's insistence on the Philippines campaign was considered futile in military circles and when the war came to an end, contributed to the decline in his popularity. Although he established an equestrian style strategy, his attachment to territory, as far as the Philippines was concerned, has counted against him.

PEASANT SOWS THE SEED OF ANNIHILATION

Attachment to territory was exceptional in the American Army, whereas in the case of Japan it was the rule, and retreats were the exception. A spontaneous retreat from a position which had no strategic value is the withdrawal from Kiska Island (see Map 3, p. 189). A successful withdrawal was that from Guadalcanal, though that was finally carried out after many thousands of officers and men had starved to death for nothing. Apart from these examples, there were numerous cases in which everyone perished, from the commander downwards. We used to look up to these as the zenith of unswerving loyalty, as mirrors of the military virtues. Even today, if we think of those soldiers who died fighting to the very end on isolated islands or points on the continent of Asia like Lameng or Myitkyina, we are stirred to the very depth of our beings.

But that can be interpreted in two ways. The first is certainly sympathy for the soldier's loyalty; the second is anger with the General Staff who failed at the right time to withdraw those courageous men who were sacrificed in this way.

From our point of view annihilation is tragic, heroic and beautiful. But if we consider it from the point of view of an equestrian society, might we not think of it as a foolish, even pathetically ridiculous action? Those Japanese who fought on stubbornly to the death in places which had no strategic value at all might then perhaps appear like some miser who refuses to let go even a tiny scrap of land once he has laid hands on it, or like the monkey in the folk tale who could not pull his hand out of the jar, once he had grasped the beans tightly.

From this angle, some aspects of Japanese national feeling since the days of the Manchurian Incident, 1931, become clear. We were unable to take Manchuria even in a great war like the Russo-Japanese War (1904–05)[8]; it was a territory perhaps two and a half times the size of Japan. Yet, later on, it came under the domination of a Japan almost without any casualties at all. That this tickled the peasant fancy of the Japanese cannot be denied.

In 1924 the anti-Japanese immigration laws in the US made emigration to America out of the question and farming families were worried about the future prospects of the second and third sons. Although Japan became bogged down in the China Incident (1937 onwards),[9] there were many Japanese peasants who were pleased to gaze at the area occupied by Japan on maps spread out on the wall, seeing it grow larger and larger.

Even in the case of the Great East Asia War, the so-called Pacific War, the map of East Asia gradually took on the colouring of Japanese territory. There was in those days a small weekly magazine called *Shuho* (The Weekly Report) which showed on maps the clear increase in size of the occupied areas. We may well believe that many Japanese suddenly found themselves entertaining similar thoughts to those of a big landowner.

Not only the general public, but the great soldiers of the day—many of whom were from farming families—were possessed by such thoughts. But the prospect of a solution of the China Incident disappeared. Although economic pressure was applied by the · US and other nations, the supreme authorities of the army still found it absolutely impossible to withdraw troops from the occupied territories. Even when the possibility of the war dragging on and on increased, and victory was as far off as ever, the notion of letting go of the occupied territories was never put forward. What was said, in fact, was, 'Are we going to give up territory which we have bought with our blood, just on America's say-so?'

THE FOLLY OF GHQ

I remember hearing a story in a radio broadcast one day during the year the war ended, which shows how the top

brains of the army at that time valued territory which had
no strategic importance. I think it was when there were
reports that the defenders of Iwojima or Okinawa (see Map
3, p. 189) were being annihilated. An important personage
from the Army Intelligence Department said: 'On the continent of Asia, the Imperial Army still has more than a
million unwounded men under arms'. We were a people
who always looked at maps, and when he said this we could
see the undamaged Kwantung Army in Manchuria, facing
no enemy, and the large undefeated armies in the wide
spaces of occupied China, as well as in the newly conquered
lands of the Netherlands East Indies archipelago (Indonesia),
the Malayan Peninsula and Singapore—all of which were
still unharmed. It was easy to think 'Japan is not defeated
yet'.

If we can use hindsight once again, that was our peasant
nature speaking. Take a peasant family: if it gives up a tiny
patch of isolated land, the family will, if it has large estates,
still be able to live comfortably. But there is a fundamental
difference between the retention of occupied territories and
a farming family's ownership of land.

When the enemy captured strategically important positions, even if these were only small islands, then however
vast the occupied territories on the continent of Asia and
whatever the number of crack regiments you still had left, it
would avail you nothing.

The Americans did not intend systematically to retake all
the places Japan occupied, and only then land on the
Japanese mainland. For an equestrian people, the sole objective is to win the war. The top brains of the Japanese
Army, however, derived from a peasant society, and, were
focused on the area of the occupied territories which they
held.

Not only the Army adhered to this concept. According to
Rear-Admiral Takagi Sokichi, when the Navy Minister
Shimada was criticised over the annihilation of the forces on
Attu, Tarawa and Makin (see Map 3, p. 189) he replied
quite coolly, 'Don't be surprised if one or two front-line
bases are taken'. Even when Saipan was finished, the Navy
Vice-Minister Sawamoto is said to have observed, 'There
are other battlefields besides Saipan. The Expeditionary

Forces on the continent of Asia are still in good fettle and undamaged, so the final victory in the Pacific war will still be ours'.

I do not know if that betrayed his true feelings or not. Perhaps he was bluffing and in his heart of hearts knew how appalling the situation really was. Even so, what he said implies that ultimately territory is what we Japanese valued. He did not lay enough stress on the notion that what is finally important in war is to win and that you win by securing strategic positions, not by holding on to vast areas of territory.

NOTES

1. The Taiheiki, a literary chronicle describing the decades of civil strife and warfare of the early 14th century, introduces Masashige as appearing in a dream to Emperor Go-Daigo, who had been forced to flee from Kyoto in 1331 for plotting to overthrow the Kamakura shogunate. He summoned Masashige who assured him that by bold and skilful strategy the armies of Kamakura would be destroyed. Masashige established a reputation as a brilliant military tactician; constantly outnumbered and often short of supplies he held the shogunate forces at bay for an unexpectedly long time, at Chihaya in Kawachi Province, near Osaka.

2. Kemmu refers to the name of this era inaugurated by the Emperor Go-Daigo, whose restoration government was little more than an anachronistic pause between the overthrow of the first shogunate and the founding of the second. The concept of imperial restoration derives from the enduring belief, rooted in ancient myths, about the divine origins of Japan and its people, whereby a direct, dynastic line descended from 'Amaterasu Omikami', the Sun Goddess, who is said to rule the land eternally.

3. The first Emperor of Shu.

4. (*The Travels of Marco Polo* (Marsden-Wright, 1926) p. 130. Watanabe's italics.)

5. The term Gekokujo (the over-turning of those on top by those below) is often used to characterise this period. Local deputy military governors and military proprietors established control over provinces that had hitherto been ruled by the weakening Shugo (military governor) houses. The Imperial Court, the Ashikaga Shogun, the Shugo and temples found themselves powerless against those who were intent on waging constant warfare to defend or enlarge their domains.

6. He gained favour with the master of the Kiyosu region called Oda Nobunaga, and ultimately completed the work of national reunification begun by him.

7. He had been closely allied with Nobunaga before his death. His fortress on the Mt Komaki nearby Nagakute area was attacked by Hideyoshi (1584); however, he resisted successfully, defeating and killing Hideyoshi's general, Ikeda Shoryu, who had attempted to take Ieyasu in the rear.

8. The Japanese fought the Russians in Manchuria, during the Russo-Japanese war, in order to prevent the Russians advancing into the southern part of Manchuria and Korea, and were satisfied with getting the territory of Kwantung. Later, in the Manchurian Incident of 1931, fighting broke out between Japanese garrison and the local Chinese military clique which resulted in Manchuria becoming a no-man's land and in 1932 a new state was formed under Pu Yi, previously emperor of the Manchu dynasty, who had abdicated control of China in 1912, which was in reality a puppet government of Japan.

9. In 1937 the Japanese garrison and the Chinese Communist Party blamed each other for beginning the incident; however, after World War, the Chinese Communist Party made clear that this had been a trick designed by them to make the Japanese and Kuomintang soldiers fight each other.

3 The Japanese Feeling of Security: Ancestral Roots. The Soil

The peasant's life depended, naturally, on the soil. The amount he could produce per unit area was much higher than that produced by a nomadic people. So people began to live in groups. Because their lives depended on the soil they feared nothing except natural catastrophes or sickness, things that transcended man's power. They had a simple religious spirit to cope with such inevitable happenings.

An old professor of Japanese literature whom I greatly respected once said to me, 'Man's real happiness lies in knowing that he uses the same privy his parents, grandparents and ancestors used, and that his sons and grandsons will use it too'. Our parents were raised by their parents; by eating rice and vegetables fertilised by their excrement we live on the excrement of our parents in our turn. We exist in the world as a result of our parents' bodily existence. We can say our own bodies exist as a result of the circulation of the excrement of our forefathers, or, as we would say now, its recycling. Our forefathers' excrement went into this Japanese soil which produced the rice which our parents ate.

We can look back to a time when we demonstrated our reverence for rice and vegetables, when there were no flush toilets and you had to bail out your own night-soil. There used to be 'night-soil rights' and methods of bailing out excreta. The peasants who had 'the night-soil rights' paid the price in rice and vegetables. The topic may be indelicate, but the theme has very emotional overtones and we must pay some attention to it.

Human beings eat, and afterwards excrete. What was excreted was, in Japan, scattered on the fields and rice-paddies in the past. In country villages, the excrement from your household was returned to the fields and rice-paddies of your house. Rice was harvested from it, vegetables were grown. Is it not true then that our bodies exist in a continuous line of excrement from our distant forebears?

So we can say, 'We were brought up to excrete in the same privy as our parents, and we see that our children and grandchildren excrete in it too'. Even in what may appear to our modern sensibilities rather unsavoury terms we can discern a kind of ethos and the startling expression itself reveals our identity.

It seems odd, looking back, that I first heard this theory, that using the same privy as our ancestors is most profoundly linked with the feelings of happiness of the Japanese people, in Sophia University where flush toilets had already been installed. Sophia is an urban college and has, moreover, a great number of foreign professors on its staff. The person who told me the story was a professor of Japanese literature who had been born in the country, in southern Japan. I come from northeastern Japan. I was brought up not knowing what a flush lavatory was. I knew, somehow, in my bones that this 'dirty story' had a great deal of truth in it.

THE PRIVY

Future generations will be increasingly incapable of realising this, but for some time after the war, not only in country villages but in the cities, too, people removed the excreta from their own lavatories and used it as fertiliser in their vegetable gardens. My mother came of farming stock, and after she had settled down in the city, she turned part of her garden into a vegetable patch. In the intervals of doing her job and the housework, she cultivated it herself, and fertilised it herself. It was not very big, but it yielded enough in the way of greens and eggplants for us to have more than enough to eat at home. Often we shared what we had with the neighbours. Watching my mother, I learned, that you cannot use urine in its original concentrated form; you have to dilute it liberally with water.

Hasegawa Machiko's cartoons, 'Sazae-San', show us that this did not happen only in northeastern Japan. In the northeast, and in Kyūshū, and in fact throughout the entire length and breadth of Japan, we have managed to make a living for thousands of years by giving back to the soil of Japan our own excrement.

Nowadays, it would be a psychological impossibility to pay respect to the god of the flush lavatory. But when I was little, to pay respect to the god of the privy was just as natural as paying respect to the god of the well. The privy is usually called *benjo*, 'the convenient spot' in Japanese, but in our country dialect we call it *kanjo*, 'the quiet spot'. It was decorated at the New Year with small rice-cake offerings and a sprig of pine. Long ago, people used to put out rice dumplings on a pear tree branch at New Year and what we call 'rice-cake bits' were duly placed in the privy.

The rice cake which decorated these places was never thrown away. Winter in the northeast is bitterly cold and everything freezes over. The rice cakes which were offered to the various gods were put into big jars of water in order to prevent mildew and hardening and when they were toasted on the rice-cake toaster, they stayed smooth, soft and tasty. We children gave a wide berth to the rice-cake offering to the gods of the *benjo*. Usually it was the oldest woman of the house who ate them.

In primary school, supposedly an institution of enlightenment, I often had uneasy experiences. When I was in my first year, our teacher Miss M- who always struck me as very prim and prissy, and was proud of being the daughter of a samurai family, asked the class, 'What do you do when you have phlegm in your throat?' 'Please miss, please miss!'—little hands shot up. She pointed at me. 'Spit it into a tissue', I answered. Miss M- asked again. 'If you haven't got a tissue, what do you do?' The little hands shot up again. 'Please miss, please miss!' She pointed at someone else: 'Spit it into your hankerchief.' Miss M- pressed the question further: 'And if you haven't got a hankerchief?' At last the class creep came out with the answer: 'You go to the lavatory and spit it out there'.

That was the right answer. Miss M- taught first year pupils in a country primary school that they should go to the *benjo* to spit out their phlegm. At the time I remember I felt, 'How nasty!' To hawk spittle and phlegm into the *benjo* was strictly forbidden in our house because the gods of the *benjo* were supposed to dislike it. She did not get the 'right' answer from many other children either. And I think that was because there were other families who forbade it, too. In the primary schools of Japan, in those days, there were many superstitions which needed to be eradicated and perhaps this was one of them. It is probably quite incomprehensible to today's children brought up with flush lavatories.

THE GODS OF EXCREMENT AS SEEN IN THE KOJIKI[1]

The introduction of a water-flushing system is, nevertheless, very recent. The Japanese have been aware of the connection between excrement and food from prehistoric times and this is evident in the accounts of the gods of Japan. In the first book of the *Kojiki*, when Izanami-no-Mikoto (who, with her husband Izanagi, is said to have created the Japanese archipelago) gave birth to the fire-god, was burned and fell ill, a number of gods were created:

Next, the name of the god who came out of her excrement was the god Haniyasu-biko and the goddess, Haniyasu-bime. Next, the name of the diety who came out of her urine was the Goddess Mitsuhanome. Next, the God Wakumusubi. The god's daughter was called the Goddess Toyoukebime.

Let us first of all consider the deities who were engendered by excrement: the god Haniyasu-biko and the goddess Haniyasu-bime. The *Hani* in Haniyasu means 'earth'. Research has shown that it indicates earth of a reddish yellow colour, close-textured and glutinous, used in the making of tiles and pottery, for printing designs on cloth and for making cloth with the so-called 'red pattern' (*ni-zuri*).

But etymologically it has the same root as *hayu*, *fuyasu*, *hayasu*, the basic meaning of which is the luxuriance of trees and plants. Hence the original meaning of *hani* is 'earth which causes luxuriant growth in trees and plants, particularly in farm crops'. So the connection between excrement and the luxuriant growth of plant life was an empirical fact for the people of ancient Japan. The *yasu* in Haniyasu has the meaning of 'easy'—if we go by its Chinese character—and is the same *yasu* as that in *yasuraka*, 'peaceful' or 'tranquil'.

So the name of the God Haniyasu means 'the god who protects the fertility of the earth'. In ancient times, in the foothills of Mount Kagu near Nara, there seems to have been a big 'Haniyasu Pool' which is mentioned in a hymn celebrating the Founding of the Empire Festival.

Next comes the goddess born from urine, *Yumari*, and her name is Mitsuhanome. In the word *Mitsuba* ('mitsu' [three]+ 'ha' [leaf]) lies the meaning 'trefoil' or 'field bamboo' (*no-dake*) or 'Japanese cypress' (*hinoki*). The name of the goddess, however, is not that; it is no doubt 'Mitsu-ha', in which 'Mitsu' is the same as the 'mizu' of *mizuho* ('fresh rice-ears') and is from the same root as 'mitsu' meaning to be full. So we must consider her as the goddess Mitsu-ha, 'goddess of the propitious leaf'. There is a connection with the beautiful and luxuriant leaf of the plant. The people of ancient Japan knew that urine mixed with water made the leaves of plants fresh and luxuriant in a couple of days.

THE OUTER SHRINE OF ISE GOES BACK TO THE EXCREMENT OF IZANAMI-NO-MIKOTO

The child of this goddess (Mitsuhanome) is the god Waku-musubi. The *musubi* is attached to all of the names of important gods in Japan. The three supreme beings who first appeared in the field of Taka-magahara (the heavenly plain) were the gods Ame-no-minaka-nushi-no-kami, then Takami-musubi-no-kami, and Kamu-musubi-no-kami.

Musubi is from the same root as *musubu*, 'to join', and *umu*, 'to give birth', and indicates 'accumulation of things'. *Waku* is the *waku* of such phrases as *oyu ga waku*, 'the (*hot*) water is boiling', *mizu ga waku* 'water gushes forth', and *mushi ga waku*, 'flies breed'. The uses convey the idea of 'growing without limit', 'plump', or 'shaggy'. So the god *waku-musubi* shows 'a rich and luxuriant ripening of cereals and agricultural products', 'yielding well just as water gushes forth from a spring'. This is the lineage of the goddess of urine.

The goddess Toyo-ukebime is, significantly, the daughter of this god. The goddess herself is the object of worship at the outer shrine of the Ise Shrine, the Toyo-uke-Dai-jingu, which, together with the Inner Shrine of Ise, dedicated to the Goddess Amaterasu-o-mi-kami, is by far the most sacred among the shrines of Japan.

The word *toyo* in *toyo-uke* means 'rich', 'abundant' and as in *toyo-hata-gumo* ('rich-flag-cloud') or *toyo-ashi-hara* ('fertile-reed-plain'), it is used as a euphemism. *Uke* is like *ke*, and means 'food'. The *ke* in this instance is thought to have the same root as *kuu* ('to eat'). *Mi-ke* means 'food offered to the gods' or 'Emperor's food'. The word *ke* is used also in *kekoto* ('meal') and *keko* ('eating utensils').

In *uke* there is also the meaning of 'container' for holding cereals. At any rate, *toyo-uke* means 'rich in cereals', 'the cereals are abundant'. Periods when rice is in surplus, as it was after the war, are exceptional periods in Japan's long history. Everyone, from Emperor to beggar, customarily prayed for the fertility of the five cereals. So it is easy to understand why the goddess Toyo-ukebime receives especially high reverence.

Now, the theoretical side of Japanese Shinto began with the Outer Shrine at Ise. Also 'The Story of the direct descent from the sun god' of Kitabatake Chikafusa (d. 1354), 'Unique Shinto of the Yoshida Family', and the Suika Shinto of the Yamazaki Ansai (d. 1682) stand in that same tradition. That Outer Shrine goes right back to the urine of Izanami-no-mikoto. What produces the extraordinary attachment of the Japanese to their islands may not be a distinct awareness of them one by one, but the dim consciousness or subconsciousness that the soil of those islands has been fertilised by the urine and faeces of gods and goddesses with whom we are connected by blood, by our ancestors from thousands of years back; that we Japanese ourselves have received life and have grown by eating the cereals produced as a result; that we in our turn give back to that soil our own urine and faeces, and that by this means our children are born, are fed and flourish. That fact lies in the profoundest depths of our awareness. The earth of Japan *is* our ancestors themselves, and if there is an immortality for human beings, it flourishes in the soil of Japan.

A PEOPLE WHICH PERCEIVES THE IMMORTALITY AND CONTINUITY OF THE INDIVIDUAL IN THE SOIL

In Christianity and Judaism, the belief in the immortality of the soul has produced a kind of disregard for the body. In the West people are often buried in churches and an inscription is engraved on the stone above them. People walk over these stones. The bodies have turned into earth. It is not considered wrong to walk over this earth.

In the Old Testament it is written that God made Adam from earth and breathed His breath into him. When a man dies his spirit goes to heaven or hell, and the body which is made from earth becomes literally a skin which is sloughed off.

We too have a notional understanding that the body becomes a sloughed-off skin, but we want to bury that body in the soil of Japan.

Although more than 40 years have elapsed since the end of World War II, groups of Japanese bone collectors have gone to various countries which were formerly battlefields. The ordinary Japanese finds it unbearable to think that the skeletons of men who died longing for home, should bleach for ever in the jungle or cold tundra. They want to bury at least a part of every skeleton in the earth of Japan because they feel that Japanese earth itself constitutes the individual's immortality and continuity. It is true that the corpses of soldiers of other nations are if possible handed over to their families, but there are obviously many battlefields from where this cannot be done. In that case, a monument is raised to the unknown warrior and a period of silence kept in a church in his home town where Masses are also said for him. But I have not heard of any groups of German bone-collectors going to Stalingrad.

With the exception of Hokkaido and Okinawa, the islands of Japan are already mentioned by name in the *Kojiki*, and connected with them are divinities, not only an absolute God-creator, but a couple of a more human, more fundamental kind: a god and goddess. So for the Japanese the whole of Japan seems a holy land. 'It is sweet to be buried in the earth of Japan'—that feeling is found everywhere, even up to the present time.

In country villages in particular, where people use the same privy as their ancestors I think there is a deep feeling of inner security. However poor you may be, if you are born on this earth and raise your children on it, you are immortal. The most fundamental thing in the spiritual structure of a peasant people is this 'feeling of security'.

NOTE

1. The Kojiki, Japan's oldest chronicle (written in 712), recording events from the mythical age of the gods up to the time of Empress Suiko (593–628), consists of three sections, the first describing the creation of heaven and earth and the founding of Japan.

4 The Japanese Feeling of Security: Leadership and Security

Let us consider security as it is experienced in different societies. The Japanese peasant makes his living from the produce of the earth and as long as he lives on the ancestral earth—particularly as long as he uses the ancestral privy—he has an awareness of a kind of individual immortality. Of course, there are things which threaten that security—damage from cold, typhoons, epidemics and so on. But these are natural catastrophes unrelated to man's own capacities. It was popularly believed that when the virtue of the man in authority was great the five cereals (rice, wheat, chinese millet, fortail mille and bean) were fertile and when that authority was lacking there were changes in the heavens and in human society and starvation occurred.

However, as the saying goes, experience teaches that there are earthquakes even in the days of virtuous lords, and years of fertility even when the Emperor is an imbecile.

The usual sequence of cause and effect seems to be turned topsy-turvy when the ruler is hated in times of starvation and regarded as evil, and is praised in times of fertility, and called virtuous.

This seems to be less so in a nomadic society, which without commitment to a fixed place is conspicuously linked with human ability. For instance, in years when winter is early, if nomads neglect to lead their flocks of sheep southward as quickly as possible, they will be buried in the snow and possibly perish, with fatal results for the group. Such groups depend more on the ability of their leaders than an agrarian people, and if the leaders are able, will be saved and prosper. It is clear to everyone that the prosperity or collapse of the group depends on the ability of its leaders.

An agrarian people who cleave to the land find security in

it. Even so, because in times of peace it is the gods and not men who threaten their safety, they pray to the gods, they offer sacrifices, they purify their bodies. And the result is 'resignation'. There is nothing to be done ultimately, other than to be resigned, because the damage is inflicted by something which is not human.

But in an equestrian society even natural calamities can be avoided by the efficiency and ability of the leaders. It is the function of the leader to perceive that 'This year the snow is likely to be early'. When the group is engaged in conflict, security depends even more on the leader. If the leader is competent, then there is total victory, but if he bungles it, the group can be destroyed. In an equestrian society the basis of security is the outstanding excellence of the leader. So a society which prospers or collapses according to the judgement of its leader may perhaps be said to be basically an equestrian group.

EQUESTRIAN 'LEADER' CORRESPONDS TO AGRARIAN 'EARTH'

The basis of 'feeling secure' shows a marked contrast between agrarian society and equestrian society. In the case of an agrarian society, the enemy of 'feeling secure' is chiefly some natural catastrophe. By contrast, in an equestrian society, the enemy is human: 'the inefficient leader'. In an agrarian society, where life is lived peacefully, great leaders are not needed; in an equestrian society it is a prerequisite of existence itself to have a suitable leader. Putting it another way, what corresponds to 'the earth' or 'the land' in an agrarian society is, in a nomadic society, the leader.

AN ENVY-SOCIETY

Let us take a modern example; there is a comic strip by Yokoyama Mitsuteru called *Ōkami no seiza* (*The Wolf Constellation*), which tells the story of a young Japanese who achieves success by joining a gang of mounted bandits in Manchuria.

It is, I suppose, a children's story, but really it is modelled on the accounts of mounted bandit chiefs like Date Junnosuke and Kohinata Hakuro[1] who were typical of many Japanese mounted bandits who crossed over into Manchuria (in northeast China). The author met Mr Kohinata Hakuro, listened to stories of his stormy and chequered youth, and collected material from other old mounted bandits. His hero Kensaku did not exist in real life, but the general line of the narrative is close to reality.

The youth Kensaku is picked up by mounted Chinese bandits and at first made to do odd jobs. But he volunteers for a special raiding unit and distinguishes himself in his first battle. He is at once promoted by the great chief and becomes the leader of seven adult bandits. The fact that he is Japanese, is young, and up to that time has had no experience, is no problem. He fulfils his role splendidly among the bandit group who act under his command. In a group of men who have resolved to live or die in total dependence on the judgement of their leader, the man who has the ability to rescue the gang from certain death and lead them to victory becomes their chief.

In *The Wolf Constellation* the young Kensaku carries out the brave deed of opening the enemy's castle gate from within, and it is this which allows him to become the head of seven adult bandits. Do they grumble at becoming the subordinates of a young foreigner? Not at all. No doubt the comic-strip nature of the story is in part responsible for this, but it remains true that in a group which walks a tight-rope between life and death, it does not matter whether the chief who saves their lives is young or old.

A SOCIETY WHERE VIRTUE COUNTS MORE THAN ABILITY OR INTELLECTUAL POWER

In an agrarian society, which places its feelings of security in the earth, differences of ability are not as highly regarded as they are in an equestrian society. For leadership in a peasant society, virtues like sincerity, effort and spirit of sacrifice mean more than tremendous efficiency. Still more important is to be someone who does not provoke the spirit of envy among his fellow villagers.

As I have tried to point out, when efficiency is not a prime factor, we are apt to think that sparrow and eagle are roughly on the same footing. In the values of an equestrian society there is all the difference in the world between a man with a big strong body who can run fast, whose eyes are sharp and whose hearing is good, and the dull-witted man who is weak, cowardly and short-sighted. The former becomes a general, the latter is killed in the first battle. But in a village there is no great difference between two such people, provided they do the farm work of the village. In a peasant society, even differences in physical strength which are obvious at a glance can be disregarded, provided no special disease is involved. By the same token, we flatter ourselves that the same thing applies to what cannot be seen with the naked eye, like intellectual power.

Just after the end of the War, Kida Minoru published his book *A Tour Round a Mad Village*.[2] It is a classic masterpiece which depicts in great detail and with a sense of humour the life of people in a small agricultural village near Hachioji, about 50 kilometres from Nihonbashi, the supposed centre of Tokyo.

What is recorded in that book corresponds exactly to what I know of the countryside in the northeast of Japan. And is it not, I ask myself, the very prototype of Japanese agrarian society? Among the characters in the book the reader will discover images of his own friends and acquaintances, perhaps even of himself. One chapter is called 'How to govern without authority'.[3] In it the author describes those who decide the fate of the village: the schoolteacher Tamura and the old man Kizaki are both over 60, both of them suffer from high blood pressure, are troubled with paralysis and both walk with the gait of a mechanical toy. Two anecdotes about them reveal the stupidity of these old men. The old chap Kizaki loved big radishes, and he insisted on growing them himself, leaving other vegetables to other people's care. One autumn the radishes in old Kizaki's patch did not sprout. He went off to Sadanii, who had given him the seeds, thinking perhaps the cause was their poor quality. But Sadanii's radishes were putting out perfect shoots. The young daughter-in-law Miechan came to where they were puzzling the matter out, went off to the store rooms, which were full of sacks, and found a paper parcel containing radish seeds. It had been lying there ever since Sadanii gave it to Kizaki. Old Kizaki had made a ridge for his radish patch unaided, but he had completely forgotten to sow the seed. You can see how senile he was.

A similar story is told about the other one, Tamura. He had been given some carrots two or three months before and said he had buried them in his front garden. His family could not find where he had put them. 'Perhaps it was the *back* garden?' they said, and looked but they found nothing. One day a girl came across them when she was in the warehouse. The carrots were drying out on the stone steps. 'They were in front of the storehouse', she said and the old teacher Tamura was quite taken aback.

Then, 'That's right', he said. 'I meant to bury them in the front garden, and a note came from the office, and I forgot.' Neither of these two village elders, old Kizaki and the old teacher Tamura, what with their advancing years, their high blood pressure, and their paralysis, had much of a memory. In the practical business of living, they had nothing useful to offer, but whenever any item for discussion arose in the village, the entire village would move in the direction decided by those two. It was very odd: those old men had no legal authority, no physical power, and certainly no authority derived from learning.

Even so, we have to take into account the fact that these two senile elders were the only people whom the villagers obeyed, for they alone could give advice when the other people of the village were troubled; help came through them, through them alone, and similarly they were responsible for collecting most of the obligatory contributions at both village and national levels. In a peaceful village the things that cause upsets are, for instance, bad relations between a husband and wife, or such problems as a slightly unreasonable marriage proposal. What is important in such cases is that the leaders should have some knowledge of the people and both time and kindness enough to listen to someone's account of a painful situation.

Furthermore, since obligatory collection of national funds imposed on a poor out-of-the-way village is not likely to be very burdensome, two old men with time and money to spare can certainly look after them without loss of income, at their own expense. No special talent or efficiency is needed to decide on village affairs. What you need is a willingness to chat to people, to be kind, to be a good listener in awkward situations, to be generous and open-handed.

You may be a bit senile, you may be paralytic, but if you have these other qualifications you are more than adequate as a village leader. It does not matter how old you may be, or how palsied, you will preserve the harmony of the village even better because you will not be the butt of anyone's envy.

THE FEELING OF EQUALITY: AN EXPRESSION OF DON PEASANT'S NATURE

In an agrarian society, despite some differences between rich and poor, there is a pervasive feeling of equality. So we have proverbs like 'If my neighbour builds a barn with a fence, I take offence'. If there is no difference in efficiency between us, it is not unnatural to feel resentment when a neighbour's property has a barn and your own house is in a miserable state: this is the keynote of an agrarian society.

This mentality continues even to the present day. Those people who have moved into the cities have in many cases been raised in the country. You do not have peace of mind until you believe you have proved you are fully the equal of your neighbour, by doing whatever your neighbour does: when he reorganises his house you do the same as quickly as you can. If you go into the countryside today, you can see in any one village a number of quite splendid houses of similar type. If someone has a house built with a gable-board, the next man who builds after him has his built with a gable-board too. If he has a pond dug, the next one has a

pond. If he buys a chandelier, the next one buys a chandelier. And so on. This simple kind of imitation could not
have occurred in the past, because the peasants were too
poor. But these days people in the countryside are rich,
which makes it more possible than in the past to see these
tendencies clearly.

Salesmen are well aware of this. If you can get one man
to buy even a high-priced consumer product, then it is
plain sailing selling the rest. This is how Japan's domestic
electronics industry became world leader. Also, people living
in apartment blocks in cities behave in the same way. The
piano murder incident is an example of this. A depressive
who was living in a flat in a public apartment house was
annoyed by the sounds of a piano played by the small girls
in the flat below. He killed these children and their mother,
and afterwards an inquiry was instigated which revealed
that some apartment blocks had many pianos whereas others
had almost none. The explanation; if one family purchases
a piano, many neighbouring families will follow suit as
every family wishes to be equal to its neighbour.

NOTES

1. As there was no strong government in China and Manchuria in the
    early part of the 20th century, there were many groups of mounted
    bandits there. Some adventurous young Japanese men went there
    and became leaders of such groups, for example, Kohinata Hakuro,
    Date Junnosuke.
2. Kida Minoru, *A Tour Round a Mad Village* (Azuma Shobo, 1948;
    Shincho Library Edition, 1951).
3. Idem. pp. 114–19.

5 The spirit of harmony as the cause of conflict

THE IMPERIAL GHQ WHICH RUSHED HEADLONG INTO WAR BY GIVING PRIORITY TO HARMONY WITHIN THE ARMED FORCES

In a society then where differences in ability do not count, and in which everyone has a feeling of security, leadership naturally goes to the man who can preserve harmony and who is rarely the object of others' envy. All Japanese know that the phrase at the beginning of Clause One of Prince Shotoku's Seventeen-Article Constitution (604)[1] is 'Wa wo motte tōtoshi to nase'—'Regard harmony as of the foremost value', and they believe this deeply. At that time there was no danger of being attacked by foreign peoples. Fear came from discord among one's own people. And in fact Prince Shōtoku's descendants were destroyed by precisely that. The thing to be feared most by an agrarian people whose feeling of security is based on the earth is discord among one's fellows. The prime concern of the village leader is to maintain harmony among his fellow villagers. In its extreme form, this amounts to saying, 'Provided we don't split among ourselves, nothing else matters'. This notion carried to extreme limits was evident in the condition of Japan just before the outbreak of the last great war. This is instructive for us today, in that it shows what great upheavals can be caused by overestimating the importance of harmony. Again, to obtain an insight into present-day society a disinterested view of the immediately preceding period is indispensible.

It is certain that Prime Minister Tojo did not desire the outbreak of war between Japan and the United States. However, the so-called Hull Note (26 November 1941) which was the equivalent of an ultimatum from the US Secretary of State, Cordell Hull, demanded that Japan withdraw at once from the Chinese mainland.

The Americans themselves found out later how difficult it is to bring about the unconditional and immediate withdrawal of a great army in battle conditions, when they were deeply involved in Vietnam, but in 1941 they had no idea how draconian were the demands of the Hull Note on Japan.

At all events, as soon as Tojo became Prime Minister, he seems to have become anxious to avoid an outbreak of war between the US and Japan. To swallow the Hull Note and withdraw troops immediately from China was to ignore the opinion of the military circles, and with the devastating consequences of dissent amongst military and political circles so fresh in the popular imagination, this was to be avoided at all costs. The 26 February Incident had revealed how destructive a force internal dispute and the breakdown of harmony could become when between 26 and 29 February 1936 Junior army officers led an attempted *coup d'état* in Tokyo, in which several political figures were assassinated. Emperor Hirohito, in whose name the rebels claimed to act, was outraged over the killing of his closest advisers and refused to give in to their demands. They were finally rushed and the execution of their leaders and ideological mentors put an end to the Young Officers Movement and radical elements in the Army. However, the Army took advantage of the incident to increase its power and political influence and when the Hirota Koki Cabinet was installed in 1936, many policies favourable to the Army were initiated. Tojo was Prime Minister, War Minister, and a general on the active list. 'There will be war with America if we do not withdraw our troops from the continent', he admitted, 'and I am not certain we can win it.' But he had neither the confidence nor the power to manage the Army. So rather than destroy harmony within the Army, he was driven to the decision to make war on America.

FOR THE NAVY, TOO, THE SPIRIT OF 'HARMONY' TURNS INTO AN UNCONQUERABLE MONSTER

There were many critics in the Japanese Navy who strongly opposed preparation for war between Japan and the US.

Admiral Yamamoto Isoroku, then Commander-in-Chief of the Combined Fleet, had the reputation of being a forthright anti-war man. Agawa Hiroyuki's biography of Admiral Yamamoto, published in English translation in the United States and given the title *Reluctant Admiral*, confirms this. Admiral Inoue Shigeyoshi, who with him was dubbed the genius of the Naval Staff, also seems to have expressed absolute opposition to war being declared between Japan and the US. How odd then, that war occurred in the Pacific at all, if most of the responsible officers of the Fleet were opposed to it.

After meetings in which opinions hardened in favour of the advocates of war the Cabinet finally gave approval to the war in the form proposed by the Army. The Navy, too, approved it. When that step was taken, there was criticism, even within the Navy, of Admiral Shimada Shigetaro, who was Navy Minister in Tojo's Cabinet. Vice-Admiral Hoshina, who was chief of the Bureau of Naval Equipment, asked Shimada, 'Why didn't you make it more clear to the Cabinet that you were opposed to war?' Admiral Shimada is said to have answered, roughly as follows; 'The Navy does not want a war between Japan and the USA. But the Army say they cannot accept the Hull Note at any price. At this stage, if the Navy were to oppose the Army, harmony between the Army and Navy would be destroyed, and there is reason to fear that disturbances might break out in the country. If that happened, we'd be throwing out the baby with the bathwater. As the Navy can fight for at least two years, we will have ways of taking our own steps during that period. Therefore, in order to avoid the worst case—a direct confrontation with the Army—I was inevitably forced to agree to hostilities between Japan and the United States'.[2]

So, in order to preserve harmony within the Army, the decision was taken to reject the Hull Note, and in order to preserve harmony between Army and Navy, the course for war was set between Japan and the US. In other words, a great war was sparked off in order to preserve internal harmony. Quite a paradox. The military, whose function was to protect the country, slaughtered honest and decent soldiers and civilians by the million in order to preserve harmony inside their own 'village', caused their country to be turned into an incinerated desert, and were in the end defeated.

A BLUNDER: MAKING A GENERAL OFFICER COMMANDER-IN-CHIEF BY RANK RATHER THAN BY ABILITY

After war broke out the way of thinking which placed the highest value on 'harmony within the village' continued to function. Vice-Admiral Nagumo, the Commander-in-Chief of the task force which attacked Hawaii, was a product of the Torpedo School and Head of the Naval Academy. He became Commander-in-Chief of the First Naval Air Flotilla in April 1941, the year war broke out between the United States and Japan. At the time he was 54.

So, his first contact with aircraft was at the age of 54. As aircraft had been a new development in World War I it did not matter that he had come from torpedo boats, but it is natural to ask if no one else was available who had a knowledge of aircraft and aircraft carriers. But to destroy the hierarchy of rank would have been to inflict irreparable harm on the harmony of the system. Even so, critical voices were indeed raised within the Navy itself over this particular appointment. When the attack came on Pearl Harbor, Vice-Admiral Ugaki Matome wrote in his diary for that day, 'Why didn't they repeat the attack and destroy Pearl Harbor for good?' and he summed up the movements of the Nagumo Fleet like this: 'Burglar's get-away, satisfied with a little swag'.

Now that is not hindsight. That view was expressed precisely at the time when the attack was reported to have succeeded. Vice-Admiral Nagumo's own colleagues doubted whether he was a competent Commander-in-Chief of a Task Force whose main strength lay in aircraft carriers and felt that it was typical of him not to follow through. If the attack on Pearl Harbor had been repeated frequently, the ground installations would certainly have been completely demolished, the battle of Midway might not have taken place, and the outcome in the Pacific some years later might have been very different.

'When he was in the chair at operations conferences', Rear-Admiral Yamaguchi Tamon says about Vice-Admiral Nagumo, 'the C-in-C never said a word. The Chief of Staff, the senior staff officers, were a pain in the neck. Apart from the initial plan, there was absolutely no planning to exploit the results of the battle by grasping a good opportunity even when there was one, or by responding to a change in the situation.'

There was a certain nobility of character about Nagumo, and he was a very likeable person, but it was obvious that when it came to aircraft and aircraft carriers he was an amateur. No wonder he kept silent at meetings and merely listened to the discussions of his subordinates, despite criticisms made at the Battle of Midway, when the enemy's task force in the Pacific was stalking and sinking the Japanese Fleet. The village holds a meeting, and the elders who keep silent are revered and respected.

At Midway, when the US dive bombers put in their attack, the fate of three Japanese carriers out of four—*Akagi*, *Kaga*, *Soryu*—was sealed in an instant. Rear-Admiral Yamaguchi Tamon, the C-in-C of No. 2 Air Squadron, who was on board the sole surviving carrier, *Hiryu*, laid on a counter-attack, and was successful in hitting the enemy aircraft carrier Yorktown and bringing it to a standstill. It was later sunk by our submarine I–168. Then the *Hiryu* went down.

Yamaguchi and the ship's captain refused to be transferred to a destroyer and went down with their ship. Men who know the Japanese Navy well hold the view that if Yamaguchi, who was very highly thought of, had been given the position of Vice-Admiral from the start, the tragedy would not have occurred.

Rear-Admiral Yamaguchi was originally a submarine expert and after spending some time in America he was made Commander-in-Chief of No. 2 Combined Air Squadron. Even in the Japanese Task Force, Yamaguchi's No. 2 Air Squadron had the reputation of being of a particularly high standard, the result of nearly two and a half years spent in command training. So, although Yamaguchi had come from submarines, he had acquired adequate experience as the commanding officer of an air squadron by the time war broke out. Everyone knew how good he was, but Yamaguchi could not have been promoted to Commander-in-Chief of the Task Force without a serious snub being inflicted on Vice-Admiral Nagumo. Why? Because Nagumo belonged to the class 36 in the Naval Academy and Yamaguchi to the class 40. That difference in seniority counted for more than ability. If, because of his ability as an air squadron commander, Yamaguchi had vaulted over that four years' difference in the hierarchy, a crack would have become visible in the harmony of the Japanese navy.

The responsibility of the Commander-in-Chief of the Task Force for the defeat in the Battle of Midway was not investigated although four aircraft carriers, the apple of Japan's eye, were lost; as were most of the pilots, who had reached maturity since the attack on Pearl Harbor. Admiral Yamamoto Isoroku, who was undoubtedly the supreme commander of the whole Midway operation, was not removed from his position as Commander-in-Chief of the Combined Fleet. The following year, on 18 April 1943, he was shot down in the skies over the Solomons. Until that date he held the position throughout. After his death he was given the rank of Admiral of the Fleet, and a national funeral. Both the Navy and the Japanese people thought that perfectly natural.

Vice-Admiral Nagumo, who was directly responsible for Midway, became Commander-in-Chief 3rd Fleet a month after the defeat, then Sasebo Area Commander-in-Chief. In the autumn of 1943 he was Commander-in-Chief 1st Fleet, and in Spring 1944 Commander-in-Chief Central Pacific Area. The defeat in battle at Midway does not seem to have worked at all to the disadvantage of his career.

THE DEFENCE OF MOTIVES RATHER THAN RESULTS: AN EXAMPLE OF 'AMAE'[3]

Of course, in personal terms both Admiral Yamamoto and Admiral Nagumo were really splendid warriors. On at least one occasion they showed they could almost sweep from the Pacific the might of the greatest naval powers in the world,

the United States and Great Britain. Admiral Yamamoto's
death was heroic and Admiral Nagumo committed suicide
on Saipan. You could describe them as the perfect image of
the Japanese Warrior.

Nevertheless, in military matters, excellence as a human
being must take second place. Nothing counts but ability
and results.

The American forces behaved differently. Admiral
Kimmel, the supreme commander during the attack on
Pearl Harbor, was, of course, dismissed. A front line Commander-in-Chief is naturally dismissed at once if he does
not produce the expected results even in a victorious battle.
Major-General Brown on Attu Island and Lt-Colonel King
at the time of the battle for Okinawa are other instances of
this.

What must be noticed is that the touchstone by which
duty is evaluated in such cases is by no means always victory
or defeat. The US Army was defeated on Bataan, but there
was a difference in numbers which made their defeat inevitable. When they were beaten, they were taken prisoner,
and were praised as brave soldiers. On the other hand, on
Attu, a battlefield where a victory might reasonably have
been expected, they did not succeed. The results were poor.
Here the behaviour of people accustomed to assessing
'ability' or 'results' is clearly shown. In Japan there was no
habit of thinking which could lay the blame for the defeat
in the Battle of Midway or the Imphal campaign on the
shoulders of those men responsible for it.

Both Admiral Yamamoto and Admiral Nagumo did their
best. There was no question of cowardice. They may have
been defeated in battle but their personal character and
motives were beyond reproach and therefore responsibility
was not placed with them; this is motivational defence.
When security is guaranteed, there is a tendency for human
beings to become motivationally oriented. The Americans
were more prone to use success as a yardstick. Let us take as
an example the pupils of a school who have made a mistake
in calculation. So long as those pupils have made an honest
attempt, the teacher will never scold them. School is the
place of absolute security. However many mistakes in calculation are made, no one is going to be damaged or

bankrupted. So results are secondary; the most important thing is, have you or have you not had an honest attempt at the problem?

I have met parents of a child capable of taking a prize at a musical competition who were indignant because their child received a low mark in the music results at the municipal primary or middle school, when that child was, without any doubt, more musically gifted than the music teacher of the school. Perhaps because of that, his attitude in class may have been cheeky, or at any rate lacking in seriousness, so the mark he got was 3 instead of 5. To get high music marks a serious approach counted for more than musical skills. But in the world of the performing arts where income is at stake and is directly related to ability, a world in which you always risk losing your job if you lose your skill, it is normal for the skill of the performance, that is the skill of the performer, to be high. In other words, it is a world based on results. People turn a blind eye to the private lives of performing artists which may not stand close scrutiny, because they are so skilled.

The rewards and punishments of war should not be allocated by a society which has the same notion of security as a school in a country village, but in accordance with the way of thinking of the world of risk, like that of a performing artist or a people whose social organisation is based on the rewarding of skill and ability. Not so, however, for the Japanese armed forces. Whatever the cost they could not value ability more than seriousness and integrity. Even so, relations between military colleagues were not always smooth and harmony was difficult to maintain.

CLOSENESS TO EARTH TENDS TO PRODUCE LEADERS FOR WHOM SELF-IMPROVEMENT IS MORE IMPORTANT THAN VICTORY OR DEFEAT

In the *Essentials of Command*, the manual for high-ranking officers (lieutenant-general or vice-admiral upwards) of the old Japanese Army and Navy, there occurs the following phrase: 'the vicissitudes of unit command depend on the virtue and influence of the commanding officer. Provided that a man fitted to command possesses lofty ideals, fairness of temperament, an infinite capacity for understanding, a firm decisive will, superior discernment, and an exceptional power of insight, he will inevitably be the focus of popularity and respect for the entire armed forces'.

A certain author, Mr Kojima Jo has an interesting story in this connection. When he visited the US Army officers' academy he explained these 'Qualities of General Officers' to two American instructors, who held the rank of lieutenant-colonel.

As he expounded to them what was meant by '. . . lofty ideals, fairness of temperament, an infinite capacity for understanding, a firm decisive will, superior discernment, and an exceptional power of insight', they turned up their eyes, their jaws dropped, they began to mutter under their breath. 'They're not really Qualities of "General Officers"', they said, 'more like "Qualities of a Saint".' They had no notion that the general officers of Japan had to show such a degree of capability and cultivation. 'If you can get together general officers with such magnificent personal qualities, why did Japan lose the war? Could it be your generals and admirals were too absorbed in self-improvement and didn't pay sufficient attention to strategy?'[4]

Might we not, indeed, wonder whether the commanders of the Japanese forces were training to acquire personal sanctity rather than strategic ability or power of judgement in crises of battle? Did they indeed neglect strategy because of their absorption in self-cultivation?

GENGHIS KHAN'S LEADERSHIP DEPENDED ON COMPETENCE

The leadership of Japan's commanding officers depended on personal quality, nature, *character*. It was the same as the principle of government of the village by the village headman. But you cannot base your actions on a peacetime evaluation when you are at war.

Even after the defeat at Midway the Japanese forces

respected harmony more than victory over the enemy. This can be shown by the way the problem of distributing aircraft materials was dealt with at the beginning of 1944.

In 1942, by its defeat at Midway, the Japanese navy lost command of the air and had to withdraw from Guadalcanal (see Map. 3, p. 189). Then, in 1943, the Attu garrison was destroyed and in the south the troops defending Tarawa and Makin (Map 3) were annihilated. Admiral Yamamoto's death, when the plane in which he was a passenger was shot down, symbolised how dangerously diminished was Japan's air power.

Then came 1944. Now America's counterattack was carried out under an umbrella of tremendous air power and it was clear there was no way to cope with this other than to produce as many first-rate naval aircraft as possible, with the emphasis on the Zero fighter. However, in the top-level military discussions in February between Army and Navy ministers and the Army Chief of Staff and the Chief of the Naval Staff, aircraft materials were divided equally, on *cordial terms*.

At a time when the principal battlefield had shifted from the Solomons to the Marianas (see Map 3), it was sheer lunacy for Japan to pour half the little material she had into the construction of Army planes that could not fly over the sea or attack enemy transport vessels. In fact the Army ordered 2000 more planes than the Navy.

In the minds of the Army and Navy chiefs, harmony between Army and Navy seems to have been considered much more important than a victory over America; no disturbance was to be created by such questions as the sharing out of aircraft construction materials. Once again Japan's soldiers, sailors and civilians were sacrificed on the altar of the spirit which valued, above anything else, harmony between Army and Navy.

A HISTORICAL PARADOX: HARMONY PRODUCES DISHARMONY

In contrast, what happened in America? In the US an effective plan to reach the objective, victory, was chosen with speed. There is no further need to be anxious about preserving harmony, once your criterion is the most effective means of achieving the objective. Everything is directed towards the main aim, and that is pre-eminently an idea proper to a society which has long lost its peasant roots.

As soon as the Americans studied the Japanese victories at Hawaii and in Malayan waters and realised the importance of air power, they firmly placed their air forces at the centre of their priorities. The number of aircraft planned for 1942 was 60 000 (actual production 47 800 aircraft), for 1943, 125 000 (actual production 90 000); so numbers were more than doubled. The improvement in efficiency was startling. Cooperation between Army and Navy was excellent and harmony was—ironically—far better preserved than in the Japanese forces which made a fetish of harmony alone.

For example, on 18 April 1942, not quite two months before the Battle of Midway, an air attack on Japan was carried out by the 16th Task Force under the command of Vice-Admiral Halsey. The aircraft used in this raid were 'North American B25 bombers' and these were *Army* planes. The flight commander, Doolittle, was an *Army* lieutenant-colonel and the crews were volunteers from the *Army* Air Force. Even in the Navy, in a task force unconnected with the land, command of Army planes was given to Army officers. People who know the old Japanese forces are well aware that such an arrangement could not have existed in the case of Japan, not in their wildest dreams.

In November 1944, to quote another instance, when the US Navy landed in Leyte Gulf and the war was in its penultimate stages, Vice-Admiral Onishi Takijiro, Vice-Chief of the General Air Weapons Bureau at the Ministry of Munitions, and an enthusiastic apostle of the unification of Army and Navy air forces said, 'This is no time to *tangle with the Army*, and I don't intend to do so [Watanabe's italics]. He merely explained his plans; he did not urge them on anyone.[5]

In mentioning Vice-Admiral Onishi, we are speaking of the man who became the very pattern of the warrior, who committed suicide by cutting his belly open as soon as he knew Japan was defeated. This man, too, facing the decisive battle of the Philippines, feared a conflict with the Army.

We cannot help supposing that a struggle with the Army of his own country took precedence in his mind over fighting the Americans.

We should also consider here Cirtos E. Lemay, the commanding officer of the US 21 Bomber group which had its main base in the Marianas. Some time ago I wanted to find out more about the Japanese forces in war-time and enquired of Mr Genda Minoru (now a Diet member), one of the ablest men in the Japanese Fleet Air Arm, 'Who was your toughest enemy?' I had expected that Admiral Spruance's name would spring to his mind, as the victor of Midway and the Commander-in-Chief of the 16th Task Force; but I was wrong. 'The toughest enemy was Lemay', was Genda's answer.

Lemay was the man who developed the B29 bombing strategy which devastated the whole of Japan. He had entered the Army Air Force in 1928, at the age of 22, and did not belong to any elite corps of the kind you would find in the Japanese Military Academy. As a bomber formation commander he had shown his mettle in Europe and had evolved a new kind of bomber strategy. The good results of this were noticed and he became Chief of the Air Staff.

In Japan it would have been unthinkable for someone who had not been to the Military Academy or Army College—or the corresponding Navy institutions—to become Army Chief of Staff or Chief of the Naval Staff. If a man who was a student soldier in Japan became Chief of the Imperial General Staff, harmony would be disturbed, regular officers would be uncooperative and show resentment.

'RESPECT FOR HARMONY' IN INVERSE PROPORTION TO 'RESPECT FOR ABILITY'

'Respect for harmony' and 'respect for ability' do indeed seem to be in inverse proportion to one another. Because we are a society in which ability is often regarded as a hindrance, we value only the preservation of harmony, and neglect ability. This is a real problem.

Since this problem can be best observed in the course of

the last war, let us take that as an example once again, although the pattern ought to be recognisable anywhere in Japan.

After the Russo-Japanese War (1904–05), neither the Army nor the Navy had much to fear from any enemy, and since the end of that war practically nobody had been promoted because of conspicuous ability in time of war. Promotion was based on the examination results in the Military Academy or the Naval Academy, or the Army College or the Navy College. And in peace time also, the advancement of officers depended on this system, which was considered to involve the least friction; given the dynamics of envy in a culture where ability was not so rewarded, there was probably no alternative.

Moreover, since the method corresponded quite well to the nature of the Japanese people, the way of thinking described as 'preserving harmony' continued even in times of emergency, just as it had in times of peace. A long-service hierarchy which relied on seniority continued to prevail under the illusion that it was a hierarchy of ability, and finally sight was lost of the real issue—defeat or victory for Japan.

Rear-Admiral Takagi Sokichi wonders whether Admiral Yamamoto Isoroku was an exception and the only general officer to show real leadership, combining his position according to the principles of hierarchical promotion, with true innate ability. All the books and memoranda of Admiral Takagi show quite clearly, almost *ad nauseam*, that after the death of Admiral Yamamoto, promotion occurred simply according to position in the hierarchy.

In February 1943, more than half a year had elapsed since the Battle of Midway, our forces had had to withdraw from Guadalcanal, and the German Army had surrendered at Stalingrad. It was a period in which, even on the field of battle, those ominous symptoms which presage defeat appeared. In April of that same year Admiral Yamamoto Isoroku died and in May the Japanese forces on Attu were wiped out.

However, in June, three men were raised to the highest rank: Admiral Nagano to Admiral of the Fleet, and the Army generals Terauchi and Sugiyama to Field Marshals.

Rear-Admiral Takagi criticises this severely: 'We witnessed a scene, shameful in war-time, of the promotion to Field Marshal or Admiral of the Fleet, of ineffective and senile generals and an admiral in whom, moreover, the Emperor did not place all that much trust'.[6]

On 22 December 1943 Rear-Admiral Takagi was invited to a meeting and dinner at the official residence of the Chief of Naval Staff, in Kasumigaseki. Japan's military situation having so seriously degenerated, he expected that the results of the studies at the Naval College and the new ideas arising from them would be put on the agenda of the meeting. He was bitterly disappointed to find that the meeting was really nothing but an ordinary banquet. He says it was a banquet to celebrate the promotion of Nagano to Admiral of the Fleet. The whole thing ended up in a one-man show of self-satisfaction and in a speech by Admiral of the Fleet Nagano, which was from start to finish a paean of praise for a private individual at the expense of the Naval General Staff. The topic of his speech was his personal rise through the hierarchical system, which had been somewhat speedier than that of two new Field Marshals.

Nagano referred to the confusion caused by the order in which names of the three who had been raised to Field Marshal rank had been published in the Official Gazette. The promotion of the three was in the order Nagano, Terauchi, Sugiyama, that is, the order of their precedence in the Supreme Military Council, so, naturally, the order of precedence in publication should follow the sequence in which they became generals or admirals. This was Nagano's case, and he obtained its recognition by the Cabinet and the Army. However, from the point of view of age, Terauchi was born in August 1879, Sugiyama in January 1880, and Nagano in June 1882, and seniority by age and the order of names in the Official Gazette was quite different from that of precedence in the Supreme Military Council. This of all things was what he was boasting about, their unhierarchical jumping of the queue.

Then this longest serving regular naval officer, now Admiral of the Fleet, returned to his home village, leaving Tokyo laden with honours. All this was utterly remote from what was happening in the war itself. On 25 November, one month before that banquet, the garrisons of Makin and Tarawa had fought practically to the last man, and the Navy had lost Rear-Admiral Shibasaki Keiji there. So there was precious little cause for a boastful speech celebrating promotion from the mouth of one of those responsible for these disasters.

Yet for a long period the feeling of security in men who were promoted by seniority was basic, and their joy in climbing to the top of the hierarchy was enough to overcome their grief over the deaths of brave men, the destroyed troops of the Navy's marines, in the main battlefield of the Pacific.

A STRANGE SCENE: A GROUP OF INEFFICIENT MEN AT THE SUMMIT OF THE SENIORITY SYSTEM

Although they are very aware of the dangers associated with promotion by ability, men who have been promoted by seniority tend by contrast to become insensitive to the basic dangers of their own system. The setting up of the Maritime Defence GHQ in November 1943 is another dreadful story. Two years after the start of the war, shipping losses had far exceeded the anticipations of the Naval General Staff and were rapidly getting worse. In spite of this, they had not apparently considered any counter-measures or any strengthening of the system. Admiral Oikawa Koshiro became the Commander-in-Chief of that GHQ.

Admiral Oikawa was the best informed man in the Navy in the Showa period (from 1926 to the present time) and, they say, had character and moral influence. But he was not inventive or ingenious enough to devise plans which could tide the Japanese forces over a difficult situation.

Transport ships were being sunk one after another; troops sent to the front line were becoming food for fishes, and, even if they did arrive at the front safely, supplies did not reach them, so they wandered around on the verge of starvation. Supplies of raw materials had come to a halt. Naturally, production in Japan did not rise. At such a time, when Japan's efforts both on the field of battle and on the home front were being strangulated, Rear-Admiral Oikawa, the Commander-in-Chief of Japan's Maritime Defence, had a special iron lectern fixed up in his office, and spent his time reading the *Gigen Shobuki* (a rare book about Chinese history, written by a Chinese scholar about a century ago) at a leisurely pace.[7] I have already referred to the instructors at the US Military Academy who had had explained to them the basic teachings of the Japanese '*Essentials of Command*' and who reacted by saying that Japan's generals and admirals paid too much attention to self-improvement and too little to strategy. There certainly seem to be plenty of examples to show that the top men in the Japanese forces were spiritual self-improvers rather than war professionals: 'In war-time, when you need the ability to take drastic measures, you will never be able to cope with a developing war situation, if you merely carry on administration by relying on the *order of precedence* of the Army List or the Navy List' [Watanabe's italics].[8]

Yet the enemy was often amazed that Japanese troops endured and fought on at the front even when vastly outnumbered. In a war the virtues of an agrarian society—endurance, earnestness, working as hard as you can—speak for themselves. Many Japanese in those days had worked on farms, many NCOs and other ranks were country-born and bred; they had those virtues.

Many years ago, in an interview with the American magazine *Newsweek*, an authority from a British military research centre said that the best soldiers of recent times were the Japanese, and perhaps after them the Vietnamese. He was, of course, referring to the NCOs and men, not to Japanese generals and supreme commanders. The higher you go in the Japanese Army, the more inferior it appears to the American. The difference is that between the village headman and the chief of a group such as the gang of mounted bandits mentioned in the Wolf Constellation Story.

The war continued into 1945; in March the garrison of Iwojima was annihilated, and in April the Americans started to land in Okinawa (see Map 3). Air raids on the Japanese mainland increased in ferocity. The German Army surrendered. On Okinawa the civilian population, in particular middle-school pupils and girl students, fought, and died. Okinawa became a hell, a foretaste of what the main islands would become if ever the battle for Japan itself took place. The Japanese people, as the slogan put it, would die honourably in their millions.

Faced by this the leaders of Japan should naturally have considered how to stem this terrible tide by examining the basic causes. But they did not.

Day after day, valuable time was wasted on lengthy official war communiqués and formal discussions, and as the mild spring weather continued, they seemed to be considering how the war affected other countries. Yet the greatest and most urgent problems lay before them, piled up like mountains: the basic control of government and home affairs, the numbers of the armed forces, decisions about battle grounds, timing plans.

Even when Saipan was taken, even after Leyte was lost, after the Americans had entered Manila (see Map 3, p. 189), and the situation in Okinawa looked grim, the top men of our Imperial General Headquarters showed no reaction at all. The members of the Supreme War Council spent day after day studying the amount of an additional rice ration for a sampan coolie and whether you could load a truck on to a *kampu* ferry.[9]

The proper role of the war leaders should have been seriously to study the chances of the battle for mainland Japan. The look in their eyes should have been different, their faces pale. Instead they behaved as if it were still peace time and they were discussing a war in some foreign country.

It was rather like an elders' meeting in a village in the mountains. As Takagi Sokichi shows, they spent time investigating in great earnestness some trivial problem hardly worth mentioning: by how many *shaku* per day you could increase the rice ration for a sampan coolie (the *shaku* is 0.0381 US pint).

It is extremely revealing that by the time you reach the summit of that kind of seniority system, that is the sort of man you have become. Men who came top in the Military Academy examinations and carried out their peace-time duty faultlessly proved to be inadequate at a time when the real enemy was attacking in strength.

NOTES

1. Prince Shotoku (574–622), statesman of the Asuka period (end of the sixth century to 710), is best remembered for his devotion to Buddhism, which he sought to extend as a religious and civilising influence over the people of Japan. As regent for the Empress Suiko, he instituted various measures to centralise the government and strengthen imperial authority, of which the Seventeen-Article Constitution is one, 'Constitution' meaning in this case a 'splendid law'. It was a highly literary text with numerous quotations from Confucian, Buddhist and Chinese writings, which was more a set of moral and political precepts.
2. Conversation reported by Professor Koyama Kenichi.
3. The term 'amae' implies that understanding can be expected from another party, even taken for granted, as between mother and child.
4. Preface to Kojima Jo, *Shikikan—Commanding Officers* (Bungei Shunju, 1971).
5. Takagi Sokichi, *Shidenteki Nihon Kaigun Shimatsuki—A Personal Account of the End of the Japanese Navy* (1975) p. 232.
6. Idem, p. 222.
7. Idem, p. 235.
8. Idem.
9. Takagi Sokichi, *Shusen Oboegaki*—Memorandum on the end of the war (Kobundo, Athenae Library) p. 32.

6 Societies in which orders are effective; Societies in which they are not

THE KWANTUNG ARMY AND THE SOVIET UNION AFTER THE AFGHANISTAN AGGRESSION: SOME POINTS IN COMMON

During the Korean war the Chinese armies came to the aid of the North Koreans, and in order to hit at Mao Tse-Tung's bases, General of the Army Douglas MacArthur insisted on bombing Manchuria (in northeastern China) and blockading the China Sea coast. He also advocated the use of Chiang Kai-shek's Kuomintang Army from Taiwan. President Truman feared that this plan would turn a localised conflict into global war and tried to dissuade him. He went out to Wake Island to discuss this with MacArthur. MacArthur did not want to listen; whereupon Truman dismissed him and made Lt-General Ridgeway Supreme Commander. Japanese who had known the Japanese Army in pre-war days saw with their own eyes how thoroughly effective orders were in America and they could not help thinking, with a feeling of respect, 'Well, they certainly do things differently in America!' In pre-war days the Japanese Government had undergone many painful and humiliating experiences as a result of the disobedience of the military.

The plans and execution of the Manchurian Incident, for example, were the work of officers of field rank in a force remote from the centre of power: the Kwantung Army. No higher commander, no politician in Tokyo, was capable of controlling it, and the end-product of that incident was a deterioration in Japan's reputation abroad. Men who remember those times reflect that the same thing has happened to Soviet Russia after the Afghan aggression. In the end, as a result of the Manchurian Incident, Japan withdrew from the League of Nations in which she had played an important part. That happened in 1931; six years later a regiment in an outlying district of North China came into conflict with Chiang Kai-shek's Army. That conflict became the China Incident, which in turn became the Pacific War. Even before that, an outlying army unit had carried out the assassination by bombing of the Chinese leader in Manchuria, Chan Tso-lin, without any authorisation and had caused great embarrassment to the central government.

The central government kept promising not to extend the conflict and to bring back peace quickly, but the Japanese Army on the Chinese mainland expanded hostilities without the approval of the government, and went on to occupy Peking, then Nanking, and the three Wuhan cities. I was only at primary school at the time, but even I thought it curious to go on calling it 'the China Incident' instead of the 'Sino-Japanese war'. A teacher at school explained it: 'It's because there's not been a declaration of war'. At the time of the Sino-Japanese War of 1894–5 though, however small the war was, it was called a war; now the conflict was vast and it seemed odd to call it an 'incident'.

Looking back on it now, I can see that it was not a war that the government had decided to wage: an 'incident' provoked by an outlying army unit is an 'emergency', nothing more. But to send a huge army, a million men strong, to fight against a neighbouring country, occupy its capital city, and then say, 'It's not a war, it's an emergency', made no sense at all.

When I went up to University after the war, I found that foreigners referred to the Japan of those days as the country with two governments. With such disjunction between government and army on questions of war and diplomacy, we can hardly call pre-war Japan a modern nation at all.

So when General Tojo, who was War Minister in the Third Konoye Cabinet, became Prime Minister in October 1941, even children felt things had steadied and settled down. Even children realised that the War Minister took no notice of the Prime Minister, so when the man who could curb the Army—the War Minister—became Prime Minister himself, everybody felt that it was the best solution.

We can certainly affirm, in that sense, that the Tojo Cabinet put an end to double government. When the head of an army which does as it pleases, in defiance of a civilian Prime Minister, himself becomes Prime Minister, opposition between civil and military will perforce come to an end. So the Great East Asia War began with a declaration of war. No 'emergency' this time. Complete strength lay with those who possessed military power. Perhaps the psychological ground was already prepared for an easy acceptance by the Japanese of a military regime since they had grown accustomed to warrior rule over a long period of their history.

Government by political parties, in which the groups who are unarmed are in control of an army with weapons, had not yet sent down roots deep into Japanese society. So to those Japanese who had seen the overthrow of governments by colonels and lieutenant-colonels, Truman's dismissal of MacArthur had all the shock of novelty. From 1929 until 1941 Japan had 13 prime ministers. Some were assassinated by young officers, others could not carry on because of the opposition of the military which was more or less controlled by radical opinions held by young officers. General Tojo's Cabinet (formed in 1941) succeeded in controlling both colonels and captains.

MACARTHUR'S PROMOTION WAS EXCEPTIONAL EVEN IN AMERICAN SOCIETY

MacArthur was no mere field officer out in the sticks. First, he came from good stock. His father, Arthur MacArthur, had been Army Chief of Staff and Governor-General of the Philippines. The young Douglas MacArthur graduated from West Point with a record the like of which had not been seen for the previous 25 years. As a young officer he acted as aide-de-camp to President Theodore Roosevelt and spent some time on the staff. In World War I he took part in a number of important engagements as Chief of Staff of the 42nd Division which he had raised himself, and was twice wounded. He refused, what is more, to be stationed in the rear and remained at the front. After the war he became commandant of the Military Academy, the youngest head in its history, and was nominated by Hoover to become Army

Chief of the General Staff in 1930, at the age of 50, young as he was. The MacArthur family was the first in which son succeeded father as Chief of the General Staff; and Douglas MacArthur was the youngest to hold that post in the period after World War I. He was also the youngest full general since Ulysses S. Grant, the Commander-in-Chief of the Federal Armies during the Civil War. His period of office was the longest of any Chief of the General Staff, and produced considerable achievements: the mechanisation of the Army and the independence of the air arm. Later, he became defence chief of the Philippines and General of the Army in the Philippines forces. After retiring from regular service, he was responsible for training the Philippines' defence forces.

When relations between Japan and the US deteriorated in 1941 President Franklin D. Roosevelt recalled MacArthur to the colours and appointed him Commander-in-Chief of the US Forces in the Far East; he again became a regular full general. He was, in fact, the first to become a full general twice. After the outbreak of the Pacific War in 1941–2, as Commander-in-Chief of the Philippines Army, he led a numerically inferior force in stubborn resistance in the Bataan Peninsula and the fortress of Corregidor for three months, withdrew to Australia by command of the President, became General Officer Commanding-in-Chief, Allied Forces, South-West Pacific, and rebuilt the US Army. After the success of his general counter-offensive he became General of the Army in 1944, and Supreme Allied Commander the following year, when he received the surrender of Japan.

It had been anticipated that governing the defeated Japanese would be difficult, because they had resisted so strongly during the war. In fact, all went very smoothly. No doubt this was due, to a large extent, to the Emperor and the nature of the Japanese people, but to carry out an occupation policy without a single disturbance required great political skill, and credit must go to MacArthur for this. Later still, during the Korean War he drove back the North Korean Army by landing his forces at Inchon. He topped the Gallup poll of popularity in 1947 in America.

CIVILIAN CONTROL

What kind of background had President Truman, in comparison with MacArthur—this *shogun* bedizened with so many victories? A country boy from Missouri who had had a variety of odd jobs after leaving primary school and had worked as an agricultural labourer, he volunteered for the Army in World War I, failed the entrance to West Point, entered the field artillery school in Oklahoma, was commissioned lieutenant after a year's training, went off to the battlefields of Western Europe and was demobilised as a major (on the very battlefield where MacArthur was a general).

Some time after returning to the United States he was elected to a judgeship in a rural court. Although elected to a judgeship he had no legal knowledge and studied law at law school in Kansas City between the ages of 39 and 41 (at the age of 39 MacArthur was head of West Point). Later, he was defeated in the rural judgeships' elections but was elected as Congressman for Missouri at the age of 50. During World War II President Roosevelt ran for election for the fourth time and Truman became Vice-President. On Roosevelt's sudden death, he succeeded to the Presidency. It was a career at the very opposite pole from that of MacArthur, who had passed from one élite post to another and had a fine, aristocratic presence. Truman had no presence, was short in stature, had not passed through the élite, and had become President by a trick of fate, a silk purse from a sow's ear.

To a Japanese, electing a President every four years implies instability: if the President is defeated in the election, he becomes merely an ordinary man again. On the other hand, MacArthur was a General of the Army, and held in his grasp the strong, tough structure of the US Army. He was, moreover, supreme commander of a force of many hundreds of thousands of troops engaged in the Korean War. How on earth could Truman dismiss MacArthur? Yet, he did, and the Japanese marvelled at it.

If MacArthur said 'No', would the Army not follow him? Surely there would be tremendous upheavals? But nothing happened. Not even a single squad of troops attempted to oppose Truman in support of MacArthur. So MacArthur was dismissed, returned to the United States, gave a speech of self-vindication before Congress, and quoted the well-known phrase 'old soldiers never die, they only fade away'—a line from an old song—to the sound of a thundering ovation. Afterwards he retired and became the president of a typewriter company. He received a fair amount of sympathy from the people for his dismissal, but nothing actually happened. The Army, in particular, created no disturbance whatever.

From a contemporary point of view, this is perfectly natural. But viewed from the perspective of those Japanese who had experience of the Japanese Army in pre-war days, the discipline of the US Army was quite remarkable. The Japanese press used it as material for a lesson in civilian control. At the time, I remembered a line from Marco Polo's *Il Milione*. When Genghis Khan dismissed generals, even very high-ranking ones, he thought it enough to send a mere soldier as his envoy. The way in which such an order was despatched is a notable feature of a society that is not dominated by principles of hierarchy and seniority.

WHY WERE THE YOUNG OFFICERS ABLE TO MANIPULATE THE GENERAL STAFF

In Japan, when the Manchurian Incident flared up, Army generals went out to investigate and returned home fooled by field officers. Those field officers who disregarded orders were promoted, in the course of time. When the Hirota Cabinet resigned in 1937 due to criticism by some members of Parliament of his obeisance to the wishes of the military, an Army general, Ugaki Kazushige was asked to form a cabinet. However, there was opposition from within the Army because when he was Minister of War he had reduced the Military Force by a few divisions, which was greatly resented by the military, and Ugaki was forced to give up. Opinion within the Army, representing the soldiers' point of view, was of course the opinion of those below General Ugaki's rank. In forming a new cabinet, the candidate for the leadership had been determined by the opinions of the elder statesmen such as Prince Saionji, and the order to form a cabinet had come in the name of the Emperor. In spite of this, the military was able to reject it. When Ugaki received the order, his first concern was whether there would be any disturbances among the young officers like those of 26 February 1936. Neither the US President nor the British Prime Minister needed to be concerned about the views of rebellious field officers and subalterns before they took office, but in pre-war Japan neither a general nor a Prime Minister could afford to disregard the views of officers of lower rank.

Tojo, who was Prime Minister at the outbreak of war, was the leader of the Control Faction (Tosei-ha) in the Army. There were certainly no disturbances within the Army after Tojo came to power. He was the man blamed for Japan's defeat so nobody had a good word to say for him. But everyone certainly seemed to have the impression that there would be effective internal control of the Army when Tojo took over. We might be tempted to think, 'If only there had been a man with the same authority as Tojo in the governing group of the Army for the previous ten years . . .' However, it is hard to know how successful Tojo's control would have been in pre-war days, since his very ability to control the Army derived from his advocacy of a warlike policy. Many voices were raised at the time in criticism of the amount of power Tojo wielded, but it was, near enough, the power a head of government ought to exercise; the previous government was in fact far too weak. It is as if the village headman and the village elders were trying to solve a dispute over water for irrigation with the neighbouring village and attempting to come to some amicable arrangement by discussion, when the lads of the village, feeling it to be all too dull and slow, decide to take matters into their own hands and end up by starting a row. The village elders are treated with the respect befitting older people, but their capacity has no backing. They cannot curb the younger men. That is how Japan was governed before Tojo.

When we consider the rebellious actions of elements of the Guards Division just before the issue of the Imperial Rescript—announcing the surrender of Japan—at the end of the war, we realise that it was very like what happens when the virtuous old men of the village are confronted by hot-blooded youth. As soon as they heard the Liaison Conference had taken the decision to bring the war to an end, field officers and subalterns attempted to stop the process and bring about a *coup d'état*. When Lieutenant-General Mori Takeshi, the general officer commanding the First Guards Division, and Lieutenant-Colonel Shiraishi tried to prevail on the lieutenant-colonels and captains not to go ahead with this *coup d'état*, Shiraishi was cut down, and General Mori was shot with a pistol. Both died. There were numerous incidents of this sort. The assassination of superior officers can occur in any army, but it seems to be a feature peculiar to Japan that when superior officers preached reason they were assassinated by raving young lunatics. In most other modern societies, those advocating a course of action which is for the benefit of the majority do not attack the position of those giving orders to execute insubordinate juniors. In pre-war Japan superior officers adopted the stance of village elders rather than givers of orders, and there was no question of shooting immediately any subordinate who did not do as he was told. We tried persuasion first. That idea was derived from the rule of virtue.

SAIGO AND OKUBO: THE COLLISION BETWEEN AGRARIAN AND EQUESTRIAN TYPES

The Army in Japan had not always pampered subordinates. Consider, for example, the admirable suppression of the Takebashi riots which broke out on the evening of 23 August 1878. These Takebashi riots originated in the discontent of a Guards artillery battery stationed at the Takebashi Gate in Kojimachi, Tokyo. They were dissatisfied with a cut in their pay resulting from certain economy measures and in their bounty from the southwest campaign in Kyushu. They killed their battery commander and the orderly officer, occupied the barracks and attempted to negotiate directly with the Emperor. They were expecting to attack their superior officers as they came on duty the following morning, but the rebellion was suppressed during the night; 53 men were shot and 118 sent to a penal colony. That was the end of it.

If we compare that with the incident which occurred nearly half a century later on 15 May 1932, we will be surprised at the difference. After the 15 May Incident, although Prime Minister Inukai Takeshi was killed, not a single man received the death penalty and all were freed after a few years. When a battery commander and an orderly officer—middle-ranking officers—had been killed, more than 50 men were sentenced to death; whereas in a calculated *coup d'état* in which a Prime Minister was assassinated, all received treatment more appropriate to a minor offence.

As I will show later, this is the result of the steady penetration into Japanese life of the ways of thinking of an agrarian society after the end of Meiji Restoration. The arrival of four American ships in 1853 shattered the very foundations of feudal Japan. In 1868 the traditional Tenno (Emperor) came to the centre of the administration and the official westernisation of Japan began. The feudal lords 'returned' their fiefs to the new central government, which act marked the beginning of modern Japan. Some of the original creators of the new central government left and raised local revolts which, however, were soon ousted by the central government's modernised army (the Saga and Shiroyama disturbances). The men who had risen to the top during the Meiji Restoration had not succeeded through virtue or seniority but through ability. When able and powerful men are at the top, punishment for those who disturb the established order of things is severe. When ability and position coincide—that period is short in the history of Japan— you have something resembling an equestrian society. A man like Okubo Toshimichi was a man of real ability at the centre of power from the time of the Restoration until his death. Witness his treatment of Eto Shinpei. When Eto Shinpei rebelled against the government in the Saga disturbances he was pursued and taken; an emergency trial was staged; he was beheaded as a traitor, and his head exposed to the public gaze.

Eto had exercised the profession of magistrate of the Edo garrison area just before the capitulation; he was the man who had proposed that Tokyo should be the new capital. He was a major figure of the Restoration, having been Vice-Minister of Education, and Minister of Justice in the Meiji Government. But Okubo showed him not the slightest mercy once he had drawn a bow at the central government. He decisively and rapidly sentenced him to the extreme penalty, and had his head exposed.

In the same way, when Saigo Takamori raised his troops on Shiroyama Hill, Okubo suppressed him without mercy. Okubo and Saigo had been friends since childhood; Okubo had eaten in Saigo's house. But when Saigo refused to heed the central authorities he had to be killed. Saigo was the leader of the foremost statesmen of the Meiji Restoration and the first full general the Army ever had. If Okubo had wavered in the slightest, the southwest campaign might not have been settled so smoothly. Because 'ability' and 'hierarchy' were at one in him, we can say that Okubo was an equestrian type of man in the Meiji Restoration government, and in comparison with him Saigo was an agrarian type.

Saigo, however, when he was young, was not the fat peasant type depicted by the bronze statue of him in Ueno Park. He was, it is said, a practical man of business with a sharp brain. But with the passage of time he had become remote from the exercise of practical affairs, and had developed into the type associated with the rule of virtue.

Part II
The Dynamics of Envy

7   The Mechanism of the Envy Society

THE ESSENTIAL FACTOR IN AN AGRARIAN SOCIETY: NEIGHBOURS NEVER CHANGE

The principle of the rule of virtue which is very noticeable in an agrarian society is derived, basically, from the feeling of security and permanence of residence. If you joined a gang of bandits, it would be impossible for you to look up to a man like old Kizaki or Tamura the school teacher as a leader, however virtuous they might be, with their high blood pressure, their paralysis, their loss of memory. Ruled by men like that, you would not survive long.

A virtuous type comes to be respected in an agrarian society for another important reason, too: in an agrarian society neighbours never change. In village life, in the distant past, neighbours (through their ancestors) remained the same for centuries. Even if it was not a state of total stability, it was a society in which neighbours did not, by and large, change all that much; and in a society with that framework much time was available for getting to know a man's character or personality thoroughly.

The Japanese have an excellent understanding of the *Analects* of Confucius,[1] because the society of ancient China, in his day, was also an agrarian society. The following phrase occurs in Section 10, Chapter 2:

> Confucius says, See what a man does
> Mark his motives
> Examine whereupon he rests,
> How can a man conceal his character?
> How can he?

THE RULE OF VIRTUE AS POLITICAL IDEOLOGY: THE CONFUCIAN IDEAL

The people in Kida Minoru's *The Mad Village* knew perfectly well that the high blood pressure and the paralysis suffered by the school teacher Tamura and old Kizaki caused memory blockages and turned them into doddering old men. But they had also known them for 60 or 70 years, and were well aware that they had not done anything unjust, were not mean, selfish or bad-tempered, had common sense, were decent men, were kind—and so on. Therefore, everyone listened when they went to a discussion and those two spoke, because no-one *envied* those old men. In this way the village was united to an extraordinary degree. It was able to preserve its harmony. Indeed, 'How can a man conceal his character, how can he?' In these words Confucius recognised the rule of virtue as a political ideology. His political theory is shown in the opening of Chapter Two of the *Analects*. 'Confucius says, He who exercises government through his virtue may be compared to the north polar star, which keeps its place and all the stars turn towards it.'

In little villages like The Mad Village that is possible. As he saw villages of that kind in ancient China, Confucius understood the form its government must take. Had he lived in Mongolia, he would have spoken differently.

In the Mad Village, after one of the two elders had died and the other had been struck dumb, three men—Gida, Sada and Yoshi—began a power struggle; the atmosphere deteriorated; the village became a vortex of discord and envy. None of these three had high blood pressure, or paralysis, and their memories were never at fault. They were far superior to the two elders in efficiency and ability.

But an agrarian society is not a combat group and it does not stand in need of strong, clever or ambitious men. What it needs is virtuous men. Once they emerge, harmony returns to the village. Confucius considered this on a national level and on that basis constructed the political theory of Confucianism.

Everyone knew about Gida, Sada and Yoshi, so the men of the village did not follow them meekly. If one man were to come to the fore from those three as village leader, he would first have to cultivate and improve his personal character. If he did not listen to others with kindness and compassion, and spend time in endless discussions with people, he would not do. Even though it might not be the most lucrative way to behave, he must never be mean.

Let time pass in this way, five years, ten years. As the neighbourhood does not change people will, imperceptibly, start to say, 'He's a fine chap'. People will listen to what the man says, and harmony will be restored to the village.

THE PATTERN OF PERSONNEL MANAGEMENT IN AN AGRARIAN SOCIETY: THE JAPANESE BUREAUCRACY

In agrarian society people are always evaluated in a leisurely fashion. To be admitted to a gang of bandits takes only one fight but to obtain the respect of one's fellow men in an agrarian society takes several decades. In the Japanese Army in World War II there were many men in higher ranks who could not adapt to emergency situations. There were discussions on why it was not possible to select efficient younger men and put the right man in the right place without more ado. But the psychological structure was such that promotion across the hierarchical lines was inadmissible.

The same seems to be true of government circles. When he was Vice-Minister for International Trade and Industry, Mr Sahashi Shigeru was a bureaucrat of the highest efficiency. People used to say, 'Sahashi was the Minister and Miki his Deputy'. Sahashi wrote a book called *Ishoku Kanryo (A Different Bureaucrat)*[2] in which he showed how the affairs of personnel among career civil servants are excellent provided everyone observes precedence in accordance with the date of entry into office, and how the atmosphere in his Ministry deteriorated when a man who had entered the service later was promoted over another with longer service, that is, when the chronological order was reversed. This occurred when Mr Ashizawa Taigi of the 1934 entry was appointed as chief secretary under the secretary-general, Mr Nagayama Tokio of the 1935 entry.

If someone asked, 'What's good about the Ministry of International Trade and Industry?', we'd probably answer, at once, that it has a bright and free atmosphere in which people can say frankly what they want to say, without worrying about higher or lower official status.

This atmosphere changed. People began to keep mum or to exchange remarks in whispers. Some began sneaking to the Secretary-General, others apathetically began carrying out work allotted to them and if someone made a clumsy criticism of the Secretary-General, there'd always be someone else only too keen to do a bit of tale-bearing. The time came when everyone felt it best to keep his mouth shut. Eventually, personnel matters made no sense; everything was done at random.[3]

Would Americans not be puzzled when they read this? When personnel management was carried out on a selective basis, undermining the chronology of entry and the sequence of long service, the atmosphere in the hitherto bright and pleasant Ministry of International Trade and Industry became oppressive. Men who belong to an equestrian type of society do not use the yardstick of long service but give important posts to young men according to their ability and talent. They would think it odd that everyone in the Ministry, given this possibility, would not jump at the chance to shine. If we ask why is Japan different in this respect, the reason is that these government officers, originally, were those that stemmed from an agrarian society.

At the deepest layer of consciousness in an agrarian society is the 'feeling of security' of which we have already spoken. Government is an organisation which cannot possibly collapse. It will go on as long as Japan itself goes on, just as agriculture goes on as long as the earth goes round the sun. When they enter the Ministry, career bureaucrats are convinced that they are all equal, in the same way that every farmer thinks he has the same ability as his neighbour. So, if the usual order of things is followed, they are promoted in chronological sequence. Those of lower rank need not be too deferential to those higher up since, however candidly they express themselves, their promotion is guaranteed by seniority. What Sahashi called 'a bright and free atmosphere' stemmed precisely from that.

Once you introduce the selection principle, the guarantee of promotion by seniority vanishes. In the world of mounted bandits, there can be no objection to the selection principle because the difference between efficiency and inefficiency is crystal-clear, but what can selection do in government offices which will never collapse? What criteria would be used in the selection process? It is by no means clear.

Anyone who has the ability to pass the career examinations, and is then backed by the authority of the civil service and the assistance of lower-grade staff, can manage to do the job. If you introduce selection, or, in other words 'being acceptable to Secretary-General Nagayama', you are introducing an element of uncertainty. Since it does not pay to have your promotion slowed by his subjective judgement, you try to avoid coming under disapproving observation and so in the end everyone keeps mum, everyone keeps his mouth shut.

THE PROBLEM OF FAVOURITISM AND THE PRINCIPLE OF MANAGEMENT IN GOVERNMENT OFFICES

So in Japan it is absolutely impossible to have the principle of selection in a system like the bureaucracy which is not subject to collapse or bankruptcy. That being the case, how do you make a decision when you only have a small number of posts to fill? Time solves the problem. The village elders, over a long period, somehow contrive to achieve a consensus, and affairs are settled calmly by men who do not sow the seed of discord or envy; in the same way calm is achieved in the bureaucracy, over a period of 30 years, by the attitude, 'Well, so long as it's *that* chap, I don't mind . . .'.

The men who enter the central bureaucracy as a career are the élite of an élite. It is quite impossible to select them by the ability principle in a bureaucracy which is governed by the principles of an agrarian society. Yet a difference gradually emerges even among men for whom it is usual to move in 30 years from junior civil servant to head of department. There is health, for one thing, which produces a fair amount of differentiation: in the past it was TB; now it is cancer or there may be traffic accidents, or perhaps defections; also, in time corruption may show up. Today there may not be any particular stigma about divorce, but it has repercussions on the nerves and could give rise to neuroses and depression. Furthermore, there are men who may be thought unable to carry out major tasks.

For reasons of this kind, when the time comes for the Head of Department to leave, there is no great problem as to who will take his place, because there has been such a long time for weeding-out. When someone becomes Head of Department, those who entered the Ministry in the same year are all transferred, or to put it plainly, they are posted elsewhere outside their ministry. And those who are to be considered for Head of Department for the next period emerge.

This system of personnel management is one in which 'harmony' is easiest to preserve. Japan's central bureaucracy is a system highly valued internationally, in spite of the fact that it operates on the non-selective principle of an agrarian society, because it precludes the defect of stagnation which often attaches to leaders in such a society: the passage from one person to another is done smoothly and rapidly.

Really significant changes in the bureaucracy may occur at such times as when the principle of selection is introduced, or, for instance, when a law is introduced which interferes with the traditional requirements of the system for transferring high ranking bureaucrats from the civil service to private companies.

A glance at the newspapers and weeklies will show that public opinion is hardening against the transfer of bureaucrats to the private sector. However, if this process is to be blocked, when the new head of department emerges, his contemporaries will not leave the ministry in the traditional fashion and the smooth functioning of personnel management in government offices will cease to exist. The major difficulty in this reform is that if his contemporaries do not resign at the time of the New Head's promotion, other promotions for those of the next entry will be blocked. This would work all the way down the hierarchy, and management abuses connected with the worst aspects of an agrarian society would probably arise. If this came about, other measures would have to be invented, such as persuading bureaucrats to retire on high pensions, which in turn would almost inevitably invite a negative public reaction, and ultimately a retraction of this alternative also.

THE PERSONNEL SYSTEM OF MAJOR ENTERPRISES COMPARABLE TO THE CIVIL SERVICE

The example of the large private enterprise is comparable to that of governmental offices in that they also are organisations which rarely collapse, and consequently generate great feelings of security and are run on principles approximate to those of an agrarian society.

Some time ago, in personnel management, there was a movement towards the preference for ability as a criteria in the process of selection, rather than the traditional seniority-based principle. One particular magazine, however, featured a story which showed how, when a company president, in sympathy with the new management thinking, began to run his company along the lines of reward for ability, deep hostility was in evidence, on all levels of personnel, against the president. The few who were clearly marked out by ability may have been safe enough, but the vast majority of the company staff felt excluded from the category of the able, and personal relations began to deteriorate. Finally the president was forced to leave the company which had been founded by his father, even though the profits had not declined. In fact, if the company's existence had been at risk because of financial loss, all of the staff would have put up with management based on the selection of ability, because the fundamental basis of security would have gone. However, because it was still operating, when ability was to be recognised in preference to seniority, employees felt free to challenge the company president on every level, and depths of hidden envy were revealed which could not be endured at any price.

Because a large affiliate of a *zaibatsu* (a major conglomerate) would never be likely to collapse, a feeling of security would reign and personnel management would be concerned with men who had spent 30 or more years with the company and would have been subject to the same kind of weeding out process as in the civil service, that is, through sickness, death, corruption, and so on. Also, in the process of selection of a company president from amongst the directors, the methods would be similar, in that they would be transferred to become presidents of subsidiary companies.

TWO SOCIETIES WITH BASIC DIFFERENCES IN THE SPEED OF ASSESSMENT IN PERSONNEL AFFAIRS

The assumption that neighbours do not change over so many decades—superiors, colleagues or subordinates in your place of work—means that it is not necessary for your ability to be evaluated rapidly. Of course, if you cannot work you cannot be evaluated. But if you can, everyone will realise your qualities in the long run; that you perform your work faultlessly, you are a fine man, you can be trusted, you can preserve harmony among other men. What is termed 'personal evaluation through time', which is characteristic of the Japanese-style enterprise, that is to say, of an agrarian society's enterprises, often seems to be intolerable to Americans. Yet in certain sectors Japanese enterprises which operate in America acquire a good reputation. For instance, they seem to be especially popular among blue-collar workers. Ambitious white-collar American workers on the other hand, often find the easy-going evaluation of ability in Japanese enterprises hard to take.

An American who has a diploma from a famous business school will want its value acknowledged at once. He thinks that ability can be recognised at once. Japanese enterprises think that you should be evaluated slowly and at length within the enterprise itself. In America people change their dwelling place at a much more frequent rate than in Japan.

Mr Kurokawa, a famous architect, points out in his book *Homo Movens* that in American cities 25% of inhabitants move every year, which means that the whole city population is replaced once every four years, at least theoretically. To oversimplify a little, one could say that you know no-one in your neighbourhood after four or five years have passed. If that is so, there is no period of time in which to evaluate one's neighbours slowly at all, and consequently, no one thinks it unfair to make rapid judgements. This is accentuated, the more élite the circle you belong to happens to be.

Of course, able men who have graduated from famous American business schools are keen to be immediately graded according to their ability. Obviously they will not tolerate leisurely evaluations of their achievements. On the other hand, among blue-collar workers who have despaired of achieving success in an ability-based society, the Japanese way of going about things may be pleasant and agreeable. Japanese style labour management takes on the warmer disposition of agrarian methods when compared to the apparent ruthlessness of evaluation by ability.

The notion seems to be strong in America that when personnel evaluation is done promptly, the ability principle is fair and in conformity with justice. This is clear if we look at the example of General Marshall. General Marshall produced the Marshall Plan after World War II, which was designed to aid those war devastated countries in Europe on the verge of economic ruin.

Marshall's military talents had been noticed from the time he was a young officer. In World War II, during the Argonne battles, he drafted and executed a plan for the rapid movement, unobserved by the German Army, of a large force of half a million men. This amazed his superior officers. When President Roosevelt heard that Hitler had invaded Poland he named Marshall Chief of Staff over the heads of 34 brigadier-generals, and promoted him to full general. Though the US Army is also hierarchical Roosevelt acted on the principle of ability first. The US Army was not disturbed by this; indeed, Roosevelt even enhanced his reputation as a great President.

Marshall was Marshall, a capable officer who had been selected without regard to birth or rank. He in turn, adopted the same method, example being the raising of Lieutenant-Colonel Eisenhower to the rank of General. He was promoted rapidly from then on, became supreme commander in the European Theatre and then Chief of the General Staff after the war.

Marshall's methods for the selection of his men is famous and he was universally respected as a fair-minded general of a kind rarely seen, who, far from bringing contention into the US Army, greatly raised its morale. President Roosevelt is said to have called people 'Mr.' or used their Christian names, but Marshall he called 'General'. And President Truman praised him as 'the greatest living American'.

When you compare the envy and discord resulting from promotions that disregard seniority in Japanese organisations, to the heightening of morale in the US Army when a man of ability such as Eisenhower jumps from the rank of lieutenant-colonel to the rank of general, the real differences between hierarchy and selection, between a country following agrarian ideas and a country following equestrian ideas, become very apparent.

ENVY: THE BASIS OF PERSONNEL AFFAIRS EVEN IN JAPANESE UNIVERSITIES

We have referred earlier to systems in industry which do not collapse; practically no Japanese universities collapse either, even private ones. American universities often do. So in America it is a matter of life and death for the governing body to scout for an effective President. The President racks his brains to discover effective faculty heads and they, in turn, do the same to pick efficient professors. If they did not, they would have no students. If they cannot attract enough students, the university shuts down. So American universities put out a management effort, like small private cramming schools in Japan.

In comparison, Japanese universities are a paradise. Only when a new university is being set up and it is necessary to obtain the permission of the Ministry of Education, is any effort made to fulfill the official requirements by recruiting professors with the right qualifications. Once the university gets under way, it is rare for efforts to be made by the university authorities to recruit capable professors. The main objective of management becomes the preservation of harmony among the professors already there. The principle, in which the first priority lies, is harmony which reduces to a minimum the spirit of envy among its members.

Let us take the case of a man who has taken a doctorate in English literature at an American university, after going to the United States straight from high school in Japan. Let us suppose this man comes back to Japan, and seeks employment as a professor of English literature or full-time instructor at a number of universities. There is only a very small possibility that he will be selected by a reputable university. Why? Because many teachers would be annoyed by the arrival of such a capable man. Teachers without a doctorate might perhaps feel awkward in comparison.

In a university society, which should be a world of ability and scholarly achievement, but is in fact run along the lines of an agrarian society, men with ability only slightly above the average are rejected in this fashion. To have ability and at the same time stay in the university means being completely under the aegis of an 'onshi', a 'teacher to whom one is indebted'. The American professor receives his salary and teaches. Though it is natural for students to have respect for him, there is no question of 'putting on an "ON"', that is of being involved in a moral obligation [ON] to a benefactor.

Japanese universities, however, are full of teachers under the sway of 'onshi' to whom very much is owed. Even if you show you have ability, you cannot expect a university to take you on. The employer has first to be convinced that harmony in those human relations already in existence will not be disturbed if an able man is brought in.

THE DYNAMICS OF ENVY IN THE BUSINESS EXECUTIVE SOCIETY OF JAPAN

If the hatred for talented men is so strong in universities, it is probably even more intense if we move into the business world. There is no success in the ordinary meaning of the term in universities, particularly in private universities, where if you become a full-time instructor you are sure to be promoted to tenured associate professor and tenured professor according to the number of years you have spent in your post. The position of departmental head or dean of faculty does not mean very much to the world at large. If this is the state of things in such a dull and easy-going set-up as a university, then it is no exaggeration to say that in a business firm where, if you do not succeed you lose business and money, to exhibit even a little ability is the equivalent of committing suicide. I came across the same advice offered in an article titled 'Smiling through tears—chats about the life of a white-collar worker',[4] in which Watanabe Kazuo answered the following question: 'My departmental head is very inarticulate. An outside body sent in a request for a lecture and the departmental head asked me to take it on as his representative. I am a fairly confident speaker. Would it be sensible of me to accept? This is how Mr Watanabe answered the question. It is a little long, but I would like to quote the whole piece.

> You should not accept. We have a very old saying, that a nail which sticks out gets hammered in, and it's a saying that we should consider carefully. We do say that salaried men should have ability which can be applied outside, but we must not be misled by such a phrase. You seem to have confidence in your gift of the gab, but if your lecture goes down well and everyone thinks highly of it, you will be the object of a feeling of antagonism from your departmental head. White-collar workers have strong feelings of envy. Perhaps your not very articulate departmental head will begin to hate you and your fluent delivery. In fact perhaps someone has already made a plan to trap you in just this way, by recommending you to your head of department. SO WATCH OUT! What you must do now, before everything else, is to find out who recommended you to your head of department. If you always seem complacent and want people to think you're a good speaker, people are bound to think you unsuitable as a white-collar worker. In the world of the white-collar workers, men of ability are highly suspect.

Now use the chance you've been given. Emphasise that you can't possibly act as deputy to your head of department. Flatter him to the utmost. That's the way to be a real white-collar worker.

No doubt this is somewhat dramatised, for effect. But Mr Watanabe's point can easily be understood. Neither in Kida Minoru's *Mad Village* nor in any of the little villages throughout Japan should you appear to have ability or wealth above the average. The Japanese company, we must realise, is simply an extension of those villages, and since business success is involved, the envy of one's neighbour is even more pernicious in the company.

NOTES

1. The *Analects* of Confucius consists in the words of Confucius, collected by his disciples, in a similar way to the Christian Bible.
2. Sahashi Shigeru, *Ishoku Kanryo* (*A Different Bureaucrat*) (Diamond-Sha, 1975) pp. 120–5.
3. Ibid., p. 21.
4. *Yomiuri* (weekly) 23 December 1969.

8 'Law' and 'Order' in an Agrarian Society

THE RULE FOR PEOPLE LIVING BY CUSTOMARY LAW RATHER THAN BY WRITTEN LAW

In a society where neighbours do not change, people conform to a different pattern of morality from that of a society in which neighbours change often.

When neighbours quarrel, one way of deciding who is in the right is to fight to the finish. But to try to fight and win, and at the same time to postulate that we must go on living together in the same village, with the same neighbours, is meaningless. Even if we have some excuse on our side, it is not an idea proper to an agrarian society to feel that we have failed to realise justice if we do not take our argument as far as it will go. It is rather like making a loan on the quiet. All the neighbours know the man who has given the loan, and the fact that he has kept quiet about it shows that he is a decent chap and it adds to his reputation in the long run.

Of course, murder or robbery are on a different scale but, as long as no one goes insane, things like burglary or assault do not occur in the Japanese village. When a crime is committed, a punishment greater than the formal punishment is inflicted because the village memory lasts for so many generations. It is a world in which litigation is unnecessary. Not to do anything which incurs a man's hatred, not to disturb harmony in the village is primary; that is a justice higher than justice. When you obtain justice but disturb harmony, that justice is not worth the disruption it has caused. Let us extract an idea about law in a typical agrarian society from 'The Mad Village' once more. 'The Mad Village' is exactly what the village I grew up in was like. Its laws—commandments—could be summed up under four headings; they were *very* simple: 'Don't shed blood. Don't burn your neighbour's house. Don't steal. Don't reveal the

84

village's shame to outsiders'.[1] Set them out like Moses' Ten Commandments, and they would read as follows:

Thou shalt not kill or injure.
Thou shalt not cause fire.
Thou shalt not steal.
Thou shalt not go to law.

So as well as murder and robbery, two other things, causing fire and going to law, cannot be permitted if you think of the future of a village in an unchanging social framework, where families live side by side generation after generation.

If you broke the second commandment and burned your neighbour's house by starting a fire, it would be impossible ever to look your neighbour in the face again since this was a time of no fire insurance and no possibility of compensation. The members of a family which had caused destruction by fire would have had to leave the village. In my neck of the woods, even if you ended up by burning only your own house and no one else's, you, the owner of the burnt property, went from house to house throughout the village, bare-foot, and prostrated yourself on the ground to apologise; and afterwards for three generations your family was not on an equal footing with the other villagers. Those who were known as 'the family that started the fire' were forced to feel humiliated, right down to the grandchildren of those responsible.

This harshness was, obviously, due to the fact that houses in the country were thatched and caught fire easily. What is more, the house was your only capital so a fire was something greatly to be feared and great disgrace attached to people careless enough to cause one.

FONDNESS FOR LITIGATION DISTURBS 'HARMONY': PUNISHMENT BY OSTRACISM

From our present point of view, what is probably hardest to grasp are the rules, 'don't reveal the village's shame to outsiders' and 'don't go in for lawsuits'. Because a small village resembles nothing so much as a small family, to go to law is not fitting. If you and your ancestors have acted in cooperation for generations, in a spirit of reverence for harmony, you have been, literally, exercising the ability to govern yourselves. Disputes were settled at a point of mutual tolerance, where no very deep hatred remained between neighbours, and you deliberately refrained from going to law in the magistrates' court, the police station or the court-room.

But, of course, some people have a fondness for going to law. In the 'Mad Village', too, there was a man called 'Mr Steel' (Tessan) who made a direct appeal to the village policeman about the village people. As a result none would speak to him. When Kida Minoru asked 'Mr Steel' why he went to law against the entire village, 'I went to law', was the reply, 'because the country's stronger than the village; but the village beat me.'

You may win in a court of law, and you may gain some material advantage, but if, in doing so, you break up the harmony of the whole village, then you have lost. So unless the case were so important that the very basis of your life depended on it—for instance, the seizure by a half-brother of the right to succession to the headship of the family—no one went to law.

Not a few family constitutions of former times actually prohibited law cases. For example, think of the Hamaguchi family who make the famous Yamasa soy-sauce. It is an old family going back three centuries. The man reputed to be the founding father of the family fortunes left behind 20 or so admonitions, among them the phrase 'Endure patiently and await your turn; do not go to law'.

In the constitution of the big Horiuchi brewing family, who first produced Nagareyama Mirin (sweet sake used as seasoning), occurs the phrase: 'We must never forget the saying, "the peasant should never run out of rape-seed, and never go to law" '. This is interesting, because it shows there was a proverbial expression emphasising that it was futile for a peasant to go to law. The Koyama family, a family in Komoro, Nagano Prefecture, has in its family constitution a phrase *EN-SHO-GOKU*: roughly, 'Keep distant the hell of accusation'. If we paraphrase this, it means simply, 'keep your distance from legal proceedings'. Certainly there are times when to go to law becomes destructive of the family. In my country town, there was a man called 'S' who lived in a big house. We young people thought him a pleasant middle-aged man; my mother, though, held him in contempt. Mr 'S' came from a rich land-owning family in a nearby village. He had an elder sister, much older than himself, and she with her husband inherited farm property. Thereupon, Mr 'S', the younger brother, decided to settle in the town and engage in business. He had a big house built. Both sister and brother were satisfied with this procedure, and for a long time everything went smoothly. Then by chance a 'spider' learnt of it. A 'spider' is a shyster lawyer, a crook, in fact, who knows very little law but persuades people to undertake law-suits at some profit to himself. The Japanese word for it is Kumo (spider) but we all called them Kubo in our local dialect. He put ideas into Mr 'S''s head.

'It isn't too late. The law says [this was in pre-war days] that only males can inherit family property. Now, if you go to law, everything, *all* the property held by your elder sister and her husband, will become yours.'

Mr 'S' was led astray by this and complained in court that his elder sister and her husband had unsurped property which was rightfully his. Mr 'S''s parents, now dead, had built a house in the town thinking that as Mr 'S' had little inclination for farming they should try to set him up in business. They then gave their own house to their son-in-law, who wanted to farm. For a long time Mr 'S' had been quite satisfied with this. Now, however, elder sister and younger brother began a wrangle in the law courts. The sister engaged a lawyer but she lost the case, as under the old law the male's right of inheritance was absolute. To defray the cost of the advocate's fee, a sizeable portion of land had to be sold. In pre-war days ready money was not easily available, even in fairly well-to-do families. Moreover, as she had lost the case, most of her remaining property was taken by Mr 'S', her younger brother. Did Mr 'S' profit from the victory? The answer is no. He didn't have much ready money himself, and to pay his lawyer's fee he had to sell the land he had taken from his sister. The net result was that a fairly well-to-do farming family was brought to the verge of ruin.

EVEN HIDEYOSHI FEARED TO PURSUE JUSTICE BY THE PROCESS OF LAW

In former times, the common people—particularly country folk—were ignorant of the law. They had lived for generations by simple customs based on the four rules mentioned above. If a crooked lawyer were introduced into their world, he would fleece them, or, as it was put, they would be 'drawn into the spider's web'. There was even a verb, *Kubo-Kakeru*, 'to draw into the spider's web', so there must have been a fair number of such cases. The phrase 'don't go to law' was not confined to the Edo Period (1600–1868) only, but persisted until after the Meiji Restoration of 1868.

It was not only the common people who detested litigation. Even warrior generals hated to go to law. Among Toyotomi Hideyoshi's[2] dying precepts is the phrase, 'have a healthy fear of going to law'. There are instances of warrior generals in the Civil War period (1467–1585) who are not ruled by the concepts of an agrarian society and I will come to them later. Nonetheless, they were just like members of a family insofar as they feared to assert their rights by resorting to litigation.

The reason why people in an agrarian-based society dislike obtaining justice by process of law is not only that it involves interference by outsiders, but also that the lessons of experience are not very encouraging. Let us adduce one example from the present day. An old woman lived in a small house in a ward in a Tokyo suburb. The nearby houses, one after another, began to be thoroughly rebuilt. Consumer goods multiplied, people's life-styles became Europeanised, sofas were placed in guest rooms, and every house needed as much space as possible, so rebuilding went on even at the expense of the little gardens, which were destroyed. The old lady was appalled by this rebuilding boom. She was also probably envious about the next door house being rebuilt, while her son, who was shiftless, could not rebuild their own. At any rate this old lady lodged complaints at the ward office one after another about the rebuilding of the houses in her neighbourhood.

At present, when houses are rebuilt in Tokyo, it is quite usual for them to exceed the permitted height and size specified in fire safety regulations dictating what percentage per lot of ground can be occupied by the dwelling, and diminish their neighbour's sunshine. However, nobody who infringes the rule about permitted height and size within Tokyo City, any more than those who break the rice-rationing act, has a guilty conscience about it. During the war, rice rationing was introduced and even now (since 1940) it is against the law to buy rice without a supply pass-book and infringement could attract some penalties. Yet people consider that no one else is inconvenienced if you make your own garden smaller by increasing the size of your house, any more than by eating illegally bought rice every day.

But this old lady was different. 'My neighbour seems to be exceeding the permitted height and size a little', she complained to the ward officer, or 'my house is losing sunshine because of it'. The people in the ward office did their duty. As long as anyone put in a complaint, they had to give guidance in order to protect the permitted height and size regulations. So the occupants of houses in her neighbourhood were forced to abandon part of their additional building plans and felt a good deal of ill-will towards her.

Then her son obtained some capital to build on to *their* house. The old woman hoped that her neighbours would shut their eyes to her infringements of the building regulations. But the resentment went so deep among her neighbours who had not been able to carry out the extra rebuilding they had planned that they requested the ward office to apply strictly the law of building norms to her extension plan. When this was done there was almost no space left over for extra building, so in the end she and her son had to forego their plan for adding to their property.

This small incident would probably never have arisen in a traditional agrarian society, in which you are very careful not to complain about your neighbours, so that your neighbours will never become bad-tempered with you. In the case of the above mentioned old lady, however, making complaints to the ward office was inconsiderate. Although the old woman in my example was certainly endowed with the characteristic envy of an agrarian society, she had forgotten the wisdom with which that society palliates it.

'LAW' AND 'ORDER' IN AN EQUESTRIAN SOCIETY: CERTAIN PENALTIES, SURE REWARDS

Just as there are societies which detest litigation, there are others which do not. In a society in which ability is evaluated rapidly and shrewdly, when people struggle for their rights and use 'justice' as their criterion, they appear to need obvious and clear decisions. In contrast with an agrarian society, in which litigation is disliked, members of a mobile society do not, I think, appear to dislike it to the same extent.

There is no need to be anxious, as in an agrarian society, or to think, 'I'm going to be living with my neighbours for a long time yet'. A society based on a mobile population is one in which neighbours change very frequently: today's neighbour is not tomorrow's. If disputes occur, you do not consider their effects on human relations in the future and so an effective leader is one who judges according to a justice immediately visible to everyone.

This is precisely the greatness of Genghis Khan, the typical equestrian leader. Many accounts depict Genghis Khan as a fiend without pity or compassion, a perpetrator of atrocities, thanks to the influence of *The History of the Mongols*, by A. C. M. D'Ohsson and other writers who in many places rely on accounts from the peoples Genghis Khan conquered.

However, the true picture seems to be that he was able to construct the huge Empire of the Steppes rapidly because he often meted out true justice. A great empire of that kind could not exist without rigorous justice in its courts. In an essay written as early as 1915, Dr Yanai Wataru indicated that Genghis Khan was not invariably bent on going to war; that he awarded clear rewards and punishments, and put the right man in the right place. We can deduce that he understood what education was very well, from the fact that his four children all became outstanding heroes, too. Professor Iizuka Koji and Professor Egami Namio and other scholars seem to be of the same opinion. Genghis Khan seems to have been not so much a fierce reckless warrior as an intellectual organisationally-orientated man, with clear judgement. The foundation of his success was his courts of law in which justice was clearly seen to be done by everyone, and honours and rewards were distributed impartially. By this means order was brought to all the peoples of his vast territories. Not only recent scholars, but also Marco Polo made this observation. Genghis Khan, he wrote:

> was a man of great ability and wisdom, a gifted orator and a brilliant soldier. After his election, all the Tartars in the world, dispersed as they were among various foreign countries, came to him and acknowledged his sovereignty. And he exercised it well and honourably. What more shall I tell you? The number of Tartars who rallied round him was past belief. When [Genghis] saw what a following he had, he equipped them with bows and their other customary weapons and embarked on a career of conquest. And I assure you that they conquered no less than eight provinces. He did not harm the inhabitants or despoil them of their goods, but led them along with him to conquer other nations. That is how he conquered the great multitude of nations of which you have heard. And those he conquered, when they saw his good government and gracious bearing, asked nothing better than to join his following. Then, when he had amassed such a multitude of followers that they conquered the face of the earth, he made up his mind to conquer a great part of the world.[3]

To put it simply, the allies subjugated by Genghis Khan obeyed him gladly. His justice was a universally visible justice. That is what is meant by sure punishments and certain rewards. Because he expected his courts to be impartial, according to Professor Egami Namio, Genghis Khan is said to have ordered the venue of a trial to be changed three times on one particular occasion. Obviously we cannot prove that every trial was carried out three times strictly in this way but the rule itself shows that Genghis Khan valued objectivity and fairness in his courts of law. When men can accept the objectivity and fairness of a trial, their hatred of the process of law disappears. The changing of venue three times to avoid bias and preconceived ideas is similar in its desire for justice to the change of venue available today in advanced countries, in which a case may be heard locally, then in a higher court, and lastly in the supreme court. In an empire which is made up of a variety of different peoples, if the law is not seen to be administered fairly, that empire could not persist.

SHAKESPEARE'S CANDID PORTRAYAL OF A WORLD IN WHICH LAW IS UPHELD BY A WRITTEN CODE

In Japanese villages neighbours know each other very well, and their ways of life and feelings are the same. In such circumstances, it is obvious at a glance who is right and who is wrong; no judge is needed. Appallingly bad people are ostracised or even expelled from the village community, that is, 'excommunicated' (murahachibu). The word denotes a concept derived from the ideas of a religious community, but because an agrarian society is like a religious grouping which converts the village itself into a sacred entity, expulsion from it is properly termed 'excommunication'. The English word expresses this, being of Latin origin, and signifying 'deprived of the Eucharist' or 'excluded from the religious service called the Mass'. It resembles ostracism by the village.

But what happens when relations with neighbours are distant, when we do not really understand their motives and when we mix with people whose habits are different from our own? If we can no longer take permanent relations with neighbours and colleagues for granted, we cannot expect that they will reconsider their conduct or repent of their own accord. We need the verdict of a third party.

We can understand this quite well if we consider Shakespeare's *The Merchant of Venice*. Venice was not an agrarian society but the city traded with all parts of the world. People from many different places did business there and because their commerce involved risk, which in turn meant that ability was rewarded, the way of thinking was far from that of the tradition of Japan. Antonio, the Merchant of Venice, borrowed money from the Jewish moneylender, Shylock. When the time came to repay the loan, however, he could not do so as his ships, which had been expected to dock, were reported shipwrecked. Antonio had to accept that, according to his bond, a pound of his flesh might be cut from his breast. The Jew Shylock—one of those who had always been persecuted—considered this to be his chance of legal revenge, and went to law to obtain execution according to the bond. And so we have the famous trial scene. Let us look at it briefly:

Portia: Of a strange nature is the suit you follow;
Yet in such rule that the Venetian law
Cannot impugn you as you do proceed . . .

Though justices be thy plea, considering this,
That, in the course of justice, none of us
Should see salvation: we do pray for mercy;
and that same prayer doth teach us all to render
The deeds of mercy. I have spoke thus much
To mitigate the justice of thy plea;
Which if thou follow, this strict court of Venice
Must needs give sentence 'gainst the merchant here.

Shylock: My deeds upon my head! I crave the law,
The penalty and forfeit of my bond.

Portia: Is he not able to discharge the money?

Bassanio: Yes, here I tender it for him in the court;
Yea, twice the sum: if that will not suffice,
I will be bound to pay it ten times o'er,
On forfeit of my hands, my head, my heart:
If this will not suffice, it must appear
That malice bears down truth. And I beseech you,
Wrest once the law to your authority:
To do a great right, do a little wrong,
And curb this cruel devil of his will.

Portia:	It must not be; there is no power in Venice Can alter a decree established: 'Twill be recorded for a precedent, and many an error, by the same example, Will rush into the state: it cannot be.
Shylock:	A Daniel come to judgement! yea, a Daniel! A wise young judge, how I do honour thee!
. . . Portia:	A pound of that same merchant's flesh is thine: The court awards it, and the law doth give it.
Shylock:	Most rightful judge!

So saying, the Jew Shylock intends to cut away the flesh from Antonio's breast. The dispersal of justice by means of the written bond has served to protect those living among other peoples and in many cases is the basic security of their existence. This is quite a different kind of security from that experienced by an agrarian society deeply rooted in the land of its ancestors. A country like Venice which had prospered by trade between all nations and peoples could not be consolidated unless it offered that right called 'equality before the law'. Hence Portia, acting as the judge in the trial, does not attempt to bend the law in any way. All she can do is recommend Shylock to show mercy spontaneously. When Shylock rejects this, she has no alternative but to apply the letter of the law.

Antonio, the Merchant of Venice, accepts this decision as perfectly natural, and resigns himself to death. Once he has made the contract himself, he considers what follows to be inevitable. This is how the people of a country governed by law must behave.

A BASIC CONTRAST OF TWO SOCIETIES IN TERMS OF 'THE SPIRIT OF THE LAW'

Then, as we all know, comes the sudden reversal. In the contract are written the words 'a pound of flesh' but no reference is made to the shedding of a single drop of blood. In cutting away a pound of flesh, the law may be observed, but if even one drop of Christian blood be shed, Shylock's lands and property will all be confiscated by the Treasury according to the laws of Venice.

When Shylock hears this he is astounded. However, he submits to the argument and says,

> I take this offer, then; pay the bond thrice,
> And let the Christian go.

But this time, the judge will not allow it:

> He hath refused it in the open court:
> He shall have merely justice and his bond . . .
> Thou shalt have nothing but the forfeiture,
> To be so taken at thy peril, Jew . . .
> The law hath yet another hold on you.
> It is enacted in the laws of Venice,
> If it be proved against an alien
> That by direct or indirect attempts
> He seek the life of any citizen,
> The party 'gainst the which he doth contrive
> Shall seize one half his goods; the other half
> Comes to the privy coffer of the state;
> And the offender's life lies in the mercy
> Of the Duke only, 'gainst all other voice . . .
> Thou hast contrived against the very life
> Of the defendant; and thou hast incurred
> The danger formerly by me rehearsed.
> Down, therefore, and beg mercy of the Duke.

In this way, the Jew who has attempted to revenge himself on the Merchant of Venice by taking the law literally as a shield, ends up by having his entire worldly goods confiscated by the judge who has used, in reverse, the literal application of that same law.

The defeated Shylock is consumed by fury; but he obeys what is laid down in the law. Because the judge has used the contract and the written law literally he has no choice but to comply. The play's background is said to reflect anti-Semitic feelings at the time of Queen Elizabeth I.

There is, needless to say, no specific connection with historical reality, but as we might expect, Shakespeare's genius has exposed the essential reality of the law and the

trial in a single scene of his play. Of course, in modern law
any contract which contravened the constitution and 'public
order and good custom' would be invalid, but that is a
comparatively recent thing. In pre-war Japan, real contracts
for trading in human beings were valid in practice, and
American history shows contracts being exchanged with
Indians who had not enough notion of the law and whose
lands were legally seized.

However, in an agrarian society like 'the Mad Village', no
peculiar contracts would be made in the first place. The
people of the village share the same feelings and the same
way of life and because they are not dishonest, they are safe
and secure so long as they do not do anything really odd.

But foreigners cannot live with a feeling of security in
countries with such a trial system, because they do not know
what is allowed and what is not. When you have to accept
the single subjective view of the magistrate when the verdict
is announced, you may feel that you have been unfairly
treated, but there is nothing you can do. When Westerners
came to the East, what they looked for first were under-
standably concessions, extra-territorial rights and the right
to consular trials. When a foreigner committed a crime
inside Japanese territory in Japan, the Japanese law had no
right to judge it, either under the shogunate, or later under
the Meiji government.

THE MEANING OF EXTRA-TERRITORIAL RIGHTS AND TREATY REFORM AT THE TIME OF THE MEIJI RESTORATION

When we read the biographies of the elder statesmen of the
Meiji Period, what is most apparent is their obsession with
treaty reform, with annulling the right to consular trial. In
the treaty signed at Shimoda in 1857 between Japan and
the Unites States, the so-called Ansei Treaty clause 4 reads
as follows:

> When a Japanese breaks the law against an American, the
> Japanese official shall punish him according to Japanese
> laws, and when an American breaks the law against a

Japanese, the Consul-General or Consul (names of both here) shall punish him in accordance with the laws of the United States.

Inside Japan, therefore, when a Japanese committed an offence against an American, a Japanese court punished him, but when an American committed an offence against a Japanese, the US Consul-General or Consul punished him. What this meant was, quite simply, that Japanese law did not extend to foreigners living in Japan.

Such were the unequal treaties which revealed the serious lack of confidence in Japan's laws. To resolve this situation it was necessary to make it clear that Japan maintained legal methods in line with those of the West. The desire to meet Western demands is evident in the dance parties at the Rokumeikan at that time (1880) where Japanese dignitaries, with their wives and daughters, all clad in formal dress, mixed and danced with Europeans and Americans. This may seem farcical to our modern eyes, but it was deemed necessary at the time to convince foreigners of Japan's enlightenment.

Furthermore, it was considered essential that an enlightened country should have an established written constitution, although this was not the case for some Western nations, and a complete book of major laws, beginning with a constitution, was planned.

So the Meiji government attempted to make laws as quickly as possible. It hired foreign advisers and sent Ito Hirobumi[4] (later the first prime minister) abroad; everything was done in great haste. We know that our new (post-1945) constitution was made from a rough English draft drawn up by an American, but the old Meiji Constitution itself was made in order to obtain our recognition by foreigners as a law-abiding state of the same civilised style as the United States and Europe, for the purpose of obtaining the revision of the unequal treaties which had come into force since the Ansei period (the 1850s).

The Meiji Constitution was an independent constitution but the motivation in its creation was not solely generated from within Japan; rather it was to appease forces that lay outside Japan. And the Meiji Constitution was promulgated

in 1889 on Kigensetsu, the anniversary of the accession of
the Emperor Jimmu (said to have been in 660 BC), called
today the Remembrance Day of the Foundation of the
Country (11 February). But foreigners living in Japan did
not come under the control of Japanese law until the treaty
revision achieved by Mutsu Munemitsu on 17 July 1899 . . .
ten years later. Before this treaty revision, an incident
occurred involving considerable national humiliation. In
1878 an English businessman called Hartley was accused of
trafficking in opium. The Japanese knew that there was a
link between the decline of the Chinese Empire and the sale
of opium and strictly forbade it to be imported. However,
Great Britain had the authority to hold a consular trial in
the British consular court at Yokohama and Hartley was
found not guilty. Japan completely lost her case. Our people
were enraged and the Minister for Foreign Affairs,
Terashima Munenori, had to resign although it was not
particularly his responsibility. This, then, is one example of
what is called extra-territorial legal rights or the authority
for consular trials. To be fair it should be remarked that the
United States was sympathetic to Japan's hopes for treaty
revision and Great Britain was the country most opposed to
it. The fact that relations with the US were good until the
oppression of Japanese immigrants in the United States
which began around 1908 and reached extremes in 1941,
was the result of this generous American attitude at the
time of the treaty revision. But we cannot very well one-
sidedly criticise the British attitude. Great Britain, at that
time, possessed colonies all over the world, and could hardly
be expected to obey the customary laws of a country as
underdeveloped as her own colonies, where the trial of an
Englishman would have been considered unthinkable. In
this light it is understandable that there was no confidence
in Japan, where there were clearly no codified or written
laws of Western style. Also, with regard to the trafficking of
opium in Japan, which may not have been considered a
crime at that time in England, one can understand why
Hartley was not found guilty under English law.

The importance of having a civilised written law becomes
clear when the conflicts arising from consular trial are as
apparent as in this case.

NOTES

1. Kida Minoru, *Nippon Buraku* (*A Village Named Japan*) (Iwanami Shinsho, 1967) p. 86.
2. See p. 17.
3. *The Travels of Marco Polo*, trans. R. E. Latham (Harmondsworth: Penguin, 1958) p. 63.
4. Ito Hirobumi had previously studied Western methods of finance and technology in both England and the US and as chairman of the bureau that had been established to draft the constitution, he travelled to Europe in 1882 to study various constitutional systems. The writing of the constitution began in 1883 and was finally completed and promulgated in 1889.

9 The Politics of Envy

THE LDP CONSERVATIVE PARTY

Considering the nature of the Japanese people to be fundamentally that of 'Don Peasant', we have tried to understand the ways in which its special characteristics are revealed. I would like to return to the puzzle I presented at the beginning of the book: despite the fact that there was no sign of misgovernment, why did the Fukuda Cabinet give way to the Ohira Cabinet?

Firstly the Liberal Democratic Party, like it or not, is a group of ordinary Japanese who have much the same feelings as the man in the street. The logic that activates very ordinary Japanese activates these men.

Secondly, the period was one of particular security for the LDP and, as we have seen, it is in a particularly secure group that the peasant mentality most clearly shows itself. Perhaps at this point a little explanation is required. That feeling of security arose because for the first time in many years Japan was free from the ideologies of both the extreme left and right.

1917 brought the Communist revolution in Russia. Until then, Marxism had been only one ideology. Now the significance of Marxism was substantially altered by its producing a state based on a revolution. With the emergence of a worldwide left-wing in the 20th century, international socialism began ideologically to shake the foundation of the existing sovereign states. In Japan, too, frequent strikes broke out and movements arose with the purpose of overthrowing the state.

In opposition to this trend there arose the *national* socialist movements, Hitler, Mussolini, and so on. A right-wing emerged in Japan, too. The title of Kita Ikki's book, which was regarded as the Bible of the group of military right-wing officers, known as the 'kōdōha' or Imperial Way, who upheld the principles of imperial rule, is *The Essence of Our National Polity and Pure Socialism*. Thus as socialism arose in Russia, right-wing socialism became strong elsewhere. And

100

when national and international socialism clashed within any given country, national socialism was always the victor. Japan was no exception to this rule.

At first Japan's political party of that time, the Kato Takaaki Cabinet, which was strongly opposed to the left-wing, was able to enact a law for the maintenance of civil order (1925), and to stop the spread of international socialism. Soon after, however, it was the right-wing followers of the national socialism of Kita Ikki who began to shake the government. National socialism became dominant soon after the 15 May Incident (1932) and finally the political parties perished.

The political parties were restored after the defeat of 1945 and, with the collapse of right-wing socialism, left-wing socialism again flourished; many intellectuals of this time advocated left-wing socialism and attracted a following from the younger generation. Political power except for a period of six months, however, remained always in the hands of the Conservative Party, which represented the way of thinking and feeling of the man-in-the-street. The mass of ordinary Japanese continued to fear and be in awe of left-wing ideology.

What really began to destroy the influence of left-wing socialist ideology, though, was the obvious failure of the cultural revolution in China and the sight of many tens of thousands of Vietnamese refugees from South Vietnam which in socialist terms after the Viet Cong victory became a just society free from oppression. The final blow for the left-wing came when war broke out between Communist China and the Communist North Vietnam. The feeling spread that left-wing socialism would be basically as harmful to Japan as right-wing socialism had been in war-time.

FUKUDA'S SPEECH: OFFENDING THE FEELINGS OF THE LIBERAL DEMOCRATIC ELDERS

With the wane of left-wing influence, the LDP was freed from the pressure of socialist ideology of both right and left, for the first time since 1917. The right-wing had posed no threat since the war, and now the left-wing did not, either. As a result, the 'feeling of security' inside the Liberal Democratic Party began to rise. And thus its dynamics became clear: it was an agrarian type of institution, dominated by village concepts.

Things had just reached this stage when Prime Minister Fukuda came back from the Bonn summit conference of heads of developed countries. The conference had probably been a very happy occasion for Prime Minister Fukuda. It was clear that Japan had actually steered herself nicely through the sudden leap in oil prices, even though they were thought to have shaken her economy to its very foundations. Despite being the advanced nation weakest in oil resources, Japan had weathered the crisis better than any other nation.

From the time she survived the first oil crisis, there is no doubt that Japan's advanced development was clearly acknowledged by all foreign countries: she was now one of them. 'Alone in the world Japan has developed her economy nicely throughout the period of oil crisis—I'd like to know her secret.' No doubt this was the kind of thing Mr Fukuda was hearing. It must have been very gratifying, particularly for a man of Mr Fukuda's generation, to see Japan treated as a first class power.

When Japan, somehow or other, achieved the status of the world's third naval power in pre-war days, and took her seat at the Paris Peace Conference after World War I, the Japanese people were overjoyed: 'We have entered the ranks of the first class powers'.

But they knew that there was still a big difference between living standards in Japan and those of the other first class powers. Moreover, in the space of one generation, that first class power, Japan, experienced defeat in war, and the progressives said she had become a fourth or even sixth-rate power.

So this was a comeback after 30 years to the ranks of the first class powers. Japan's military power may still be small, but that is not an important problem in the world today. The average life-span of her people is longer than that of the Americans and her people's average disposable income is nearly twice that of Great Britain which was *the* first class power before the war. Japan's gross national product (GNP) was roughly equal to that of Great Britain and France combined, and they are developed countries. Moreover, Japan's growth rate was much higher than theirs. Mr Fukuda must have felt proud to be in the company of the heads of the developed countries as the Prime Minister of this new first class power.

On his return home, Mr Fukuda looked relaxed and content. And he expressed himself in the immortal phrase, 'The whole world is calling for Fukuda'. Who else, among post-war Prime Ministers, could have expressed such sentiments? The compliant people who heard them smiled a friendly smile. The Prime Minister was the face of Japan. Because he was valued at the conference of the heads of the developed countries, it meant that the Japanese themselves were held in high esteem.

Was this not a cause for rejoicing? The men of the Liberal Democratic Party, however, particularly the leaders of the party factions, did not share the same sentiments. Fukuda was envied. Japan is like a peaceful village. Who shall become the village headman? The Liberal Democratic Party members thought that affairs could run smoothly whoever took over, so long as he was chosen from the ranks of the party faction bosses.[1] 'The whole world's calling for Fukuda' was an insensitive remark. 'Has he forgotten', the other bosses wondered, 'that he became Prime Minister after Miki's departure[2] because we all helped him?'

THE END OF A VILLAGE HEADMAN

An awareness of the subtleties of human nature is the distinctive characteristic of the men of the Liberal Democratic Party. The whisperings of 'Hasn't old Fukuda been pushing it a bit far, recently?' made things easy for those hostile to him. And their opportunity came in the preparatory elections for the Liberal Democratic Party's leadership election of November 1978. The Fukuda Cabinet had produced magnificent results at home and abroad in its treatment of long-standing problems and its economic policy had skilfully kept pace with the changing world economic climate. So it was natural that Mr Fukuda's self-confidence in his own political power should have deepened and that he should be optimistic about his re-election in the Liberal Democrats' leadership election. The mass media forecast his certain re-election as party leader. In the election the following announced their candidacy: Prime Minister Fukuda, Secretary-General Ohira, Chairman of the Executive Council Nakasone, and the Minister of International Trade and Industry Komoto.

Let us look a little more closely at what happened in that election. There was a big difference of 110 votes between the winner, Mr Ohira, and the runner-up, Mr Fukuda. As a result, Mr Fukuda abandoned the fight for the final vote and handed over the positions of Prime Minister and party chairman to Mr Ohira.

The direct cause of this unexpected event was probably the skilful strategy of the Ohira faction and the Tanaka faction, but in order to make that strategy work, the right atmosphere had to be created. For that purpose, nothing was needed but the phrase, 'The whole world is calling for Fukuda'.

While they were all saying 'Fukuda's pushing it a bit far,' or 'Fukuda's got a case of swollen head', his rival, Secretary-General Ohira, lived up to his nickname 'the dumb ox', showing by his appearance that there was nothing anyone could envy in *him*. 'Mr Ar-uh ...' (as they also nicknamed him) did not show in public the slightest glimpse of arrogance in his far from clear speech. And from the point of view of seniority and career, his turn came after Tanaka, Miki and Fukuda.

With the benefit of hindsight, the outcome was inevitable. However, the reason why the mass-media forecast was way out is that it overlooked the fact that Japan had emancipated herself from the threat of ideology when she survived the oil crisis, and was in an unprecedentedly stable position. In Japan, once there is this feeling of security, you can scarcely imagine how agrarian envy begins to work!

So, the following year, when the developed countries' Summit at Mr Fukuda's invitation opened in Tokyo, the host had changed. Although Fukuda had not been guilty of any maladministration as Prime Minister, although the economy was functioning smoothly, although there had been no revolution and no general election, Mr Fukuda had to vacate his seat. The heads of state of the developed countries cudgelled their brains, not unreasonably, and concluded, 'The Japanese are incomprehensible'. We can but guess at Mr Fukuda's chagrin.

When Mr Ohira became Prime Minister, neither Japan nor the world substantially changed. Left-wing ideology received another blow from the Soviet invasion of Afghanistan. It seemed likely we would survive the second oil crisis.

The summit in Tokyo ended uneventfully. The heads of state of the world's developed countries had assembled in Japan and that was one of the most auspicious events since the Emperor Jimmu founded this country 2640 years ago, so we must expect that Prime Minister Ohira was satisfied.

THE PSYCHOLOGY BEHIND A VOTE OF NO CONFIDENCE IN THE OHIRA CABINET

Exactly these same tendencies can be seen in the fate of Mr Ohira's career as Prime Minister. Anti-mainstream groups hostile to Mr Ohira inside the Liberal Democratic Party began to make exactly the same complaints of Ohira: 'He's arrogant', 'He's got a swollen head'. 'In Japan today, anyone who comes out on top can do the Prime Minister's job'. That is what they and their immediate underlings began to think. The prosperity of a peaceful country village owes nothing to the ability of the village headman.

To point out before the general election the need for indirect taxation was not seen as the courageous act of a responsible politician concerned with the public economy. It was criticised as 'Ohira's arrogant mood'. Ohira won the election but, contrary to expectations, did not increase his vote and this resulted in the disgraceful conduct of some of the members of the party who failed to be unanimous in nominating Ohira as Prime Minister in the Diet. Of course, such conduct was only possible because there was no longer any fear of the left-wing ideology of the opposition.

There was not a single theoretical or political strategic point at issue. What happened was like a split in the secure society of an agrarian village. 'That chap's got a swollen head' or 'He's arrogant' or 'I'm not very keen on him'—that is what was said. The dimension was that of a struggle inside a village, emotionally and in terms of personalities.

Meanwhile, the Venice Economic Summit was approaching. Prime Minister Ohira was cheerful. He was obviously quite pleased. He went abroad and made speeches in English, which he spoke very well; foreigners could follow him perfectly. However, his high reputation abroad was extremely disagreeable to the village elders and the circle of the former village headmen. 'That our village—Japan—is prosperous is due to the efforts of the entire people of the village, not to the skill of the village headman, Ohira. And yet, there's the village headman going off to town, thinking he's done it all. It's not on.'

When the opposition parties came up with their usual vote of no confidence in the government, simply in the form of a token gesture knowing that the government party was in a majority, they were struck by unexpected success: the anti-Ohira factions did not enter the Diet to vote. The faction of the former village headman abandoned the current headman. This is contrary to the village moral code. People in the village may quarrel among themselves, but it goes against the village code to desert the headman of your own village when he is attacked by chaps from a neighbouring village. 'Do not parade the village's shame before outsiders' has been the tradition of Japan's agrarian society since prehistoric times, and although they themselves did not enter the Chamber, previous 'village headmen', never having envisaged the passing of a vote of no confidence, turned pale. And so they should have.

In a television interview Mr Fukuda criticised the 'arrogant posture' of the Ohira Cabinet, but the people as a whole did not think Mr Ohira was arrogant. That was just the subjective view of the anti-mainstream faction, and they deluded themselves that the people as a whole accepted it.

The assembly dissolved. Prime Minister Ohira fell ill and went into hospital. According to news stories he was very much concerned with the long-awaited opening in Venice of the summit conference of the heads of states of the developed countries. Then suddenly he was dead.

THE ELECTION OF THE LIBERAL DEMOCRATIC CHAIRMAN AND THE ELECTION OF THE VILLAGE HEADMAN: POINTS IN COMMON

When he was dead everyone recalled Ohira with nostalgia. He was a good man. He had never done anything out of the ordinary and the people were quite sure he never would.

When it was reported that Mr Ohira's granddaughter had said, 'Grandpa died because no one was nice to him', some housewives could not help weeping. When this happened the former village headman was in a fix. The men of the next village (that is the opposition parties), too, found it hard to speak ill of the dead man. So even though they had no party head, the Liberal Democrats won a complete victory in the general election.

After the election, no decision was made about the party chairmanship until Mr Ohira's funeral was over, and it was decided to get along with a temporary substitute. So for some time, without a party chairman, without a Prime Minister, Japan's state structure continued to function smoothly without the slightest hitch. Anyone can be headman of a peaceful village? Well, this time the impression was given that we were better off with no headman at all. A big country which can entertain such feelings of security is probably very rare. Even without a Prime Minister the people as a whole were in no way perturbed or uneasy.

Naturally, rumours about the next prime minister and party chairman were rife. There were newspaper symposia and questionnaires, even I was quizzed on the issue, and took part in various discussions on television and in weeklies. Nakasone, Komoto, Miyazawa, these three names frequently emerged as candidates. Although I know next to nothing about the inner workings of the Liberal Democratic Party, in Japan's present situation, in which everyone felt secure and satisfied, I could see at work the characteristic dynamics of the agrarian society, and was able to make the following two points:

Firstly, to go back to the claim that '*anyone can do it*'. Of course, if you are a first year member of the Diet you cannot, but if you have experience of your cabinet colleagues and the party officials, it is possible.

Secondly, the men of the Fukuda faction and the Miki faction are out of the running, because the village code forbids a headman to emerge from a group which has brought disgrace on its own former headman by conniving with the chaps of the next village.

However many party members he wins over, the village feeling will be that Mr Komoto, a member of the Miki faction, cannot become headman if he does not go through the purification process of one more election.

A man well versed in politics spoke in opposition to my views. 'You say anyone can do it, but a Prime Minister needs ability to become a Prime Minister. Nakasone, Miyazawa, Komoto—all three names have emerged; but has no one mentioned a man like Suzuki Zenko?'

It is an agrarian notion that in time of peace you do not need ability or talents to become the village headman. You should only preserve the harmony of the village. Some may say that talent and ability are precisely what preserve harmony. But were old Kisaki and the old teacher Tamura in 'The Mad Village' men of ability? Is it not more likely that virtue matters more than ability and that what was valuable about them was that they were men who lived quite unremarkable lives, and never became objects of envy?

One political commentator, in a book called *Thirteen candidates for the premiership*, never once brought up the name of Suzuki Zenko. He chose 13 men, investigated the size of their factions, their parliamentary duties, their skill in diplomacy and economics, and their ability, as a basis for the premiership. But these are conditions of choosing a candidate for leadership in Western society. They have little relevance to the character of the Liberal Democratic Party village headman at the present time.

A PRIME MINISTER WHO 'APPEARS STUPID'

After Mr Ohira's death the Liberal Democratic Party went in for some self-examination. How could we have been so inept? Looking back, we can understand that the disorder in party harmony started from the circumstances of the final election vote of Tanaka and Fukuda after the retirement of Prime Minister Sato. Since it was obvious that a core of hard feeling remained after the final election for the party leader, they returned to the code of the village which prescribes a unanimous decision and proscribes a majority decision.

After Ohira's death some people might have been dissatisfied with the choice of Mr Suzuki as Prime Minister, but no hatred of him lingered of the kind that had occurred in the case of Fukuda's defeat by Tanaka in a majority decision. Besides, Mr Suzuki was a man of the Ohira camp. It is difficult to resist the suggestion that as successor of the dead village headman, as a product of the same village, he was elected if only through politeness to the dead man.

In the Ohira village, Miyazawa was conspicuous and popular with the mass media; but it is the village custom to avoid conspicuous ability. A command of English, particularly, is looked at askance. There is a common feeling that it is irritating. Party members become disgruntled when the Prime Minister greets the US President directly and fluently in English. Of course, just after the war ended, the Japanese Prime Ministers had been diplomats (Shidehara Kijuro, Yoshida Shigeru and Ashida Hitoshi, for example) but that was a time of crisis in which Japan was occupied by a foreign army. The Prime Minister had to be a linguist, capable of negotiating with MacArthur directly. Prime Minister Yoshida in particular, did nothing to diminish the arrogant pose which made people nickname him the 'One-Man Prime Minister'. But he had outstanding ability. He alone could speak with MacArthur without being subservient—was what everyone felt. As long as that was so, his position was unshakeable. However, when the Peace Treaty came into effect, and we became independent, our feeling of crisis disappeared: Japan was no longer to be administered in accordance with the mind of MacArthur alone. We no longer needed ex-diplomat prime ministers whose qualifications were a talent for the English language. The prime minister prototype was transformed step by step into that of the Japan-village-elder. In the village, the flashiest member who gets on everyone's nerves is a stylish, fashionable man. English language is fashionableness incarnate. People went to great lengths to avoid the stigma of flashiness. M. M., a friend of mine, who was once responsible for the English-language courses at the Japan Broadcasting Company, while he was working for a big commercial enterprise, concealed the fact that he could speak fluent English. It is said that he sent out to senior officials, quite deliberately, texts of which the English was faulty. Although the English language is a business tool in such a big commercial enterprise, it was necessary for him to hide his linguistic ability. This applies with even greater force in a Cabinet!

In this way the Japanese premiership adopted its most characteristic form, and we had Mr Suzuki. The prototype had become reality.

It is pure coincidence, but the name Suzuki is a name used by foreigners whenever they wish to refer to the average Japanese. Madame Butterfly's lady's maid was called Suzuki. It is one of the commonest names in Japan. It is friendlier than an unusual family name. From now on, as long as no feeling of crisis emerges in Japan, we will probably continue to have prime ministers of this type. They may display dazzling talents until they join the Cabinet. However, if anyone wishes to become prime minister in a peaceful Japan, he should follow Lao Tse's prescription: 'the Lord has illustrious virtues, but his countenance appears stupid'.

After the resignation of the Suzuki Cabinet, Nakasone was chosen as the succeeding prime minister of Japan, not by any intra-party election (which had been stipulated in the party regulations of the Liberal Democrats), but by the consensus among the elder leaders of the intra-party factions of the said party. This change of prime ministers may have been difficult for the non-Japanese to understand. My theory of 'Don Peasant' explains, or I am afraid, explains away this change as follows:

Firstly, any kind of intra-party election had to be avoided. They once stipulated a rule concerning the election of their party leader. (As the Liberal Democratic Party is the Government Party, their party leader automatically becomes Prime Minister of Japan.) They elected Tanaka and Ohira according to this stipulation, with the result that the Liberal Democratic Party suffered a severe aftermath, a bitter lingering intra-party enmity each time. The Liberal Democratic Party—the Conservative Party—has been in power uninterrupted since 1948. The Government Party is safe. When this feeling of safety is prevalent, the principle of Don Peasant is also at work. No election in the safe village—this had been a long-rooted tradition. After the long government under Sato (1964–72) came to an end, the late Sato did not appoint his successor, with the result that Tanaka and Fukuda competed with each other intensely in the intra-party election for the chair of the party leader, and the bitter aftertaste still remains to the detriment of the harmony of the party. This was the reason, as is explained above, why Suzuki was chosen as the leader of the party (that is, Prime Minister of Japan) through consensus, not by election, among the members, after the sudden death of Prime Minister Ohira in June 1980. Suzuki, though he was admitted by almost everybody to be far from a bright politician, succeeded in some measure in restoring an atmosphere of harmony to the party.

This lesson was never forgotten by the members of the Liberal Democratic Party. Thus, Nakasone was chosen as leader of the ruling Liberal Democratic Party and as Prime Minister of Japan without any challenger. In the post-Sato LDP there have been five main factions, that is, Tanaka's, Fukuda's, Ohira's (which is now Suzuki's), Miki's and Nakasone's. Nakasone was the last among these heads of factions to become party leader. The choice seemed very natural. Without a competitive intra-party election the appearance of harmony among the Liberal Democrats was to be continued without difficulty by choosing Nakasone by consensus as party leader.

As far as the conservative government remains secure without any serious challenge from the opposition parties, the succession of Japanese prime ministers will continue to follow the same pattern and the consensus among the Liberal Democratic 'villagers' will be obtained in the same way as the Don Peasants of the Japanese villages of the past. Only a sudden national or international catastrophe might change the pattern. Possibilities of change are more likely to be seen among industrial and commercial companies than among politicians, for the former are incessantly taking challenges from both native and foreign competitors. The odds are, however, that most Japanese companies will retain something of the Don Peasants principle in their inner structure, and that their way of doing things will be emulated more widely all over the world.

NOTES

1. The factions within the LDP are parallel to the political parties of other countries such as Great Britain. This is because the opposition parties stand virtually no chance of forming a government. There are currently five factions in the LDP, four of which are considerably weaker than the powerful Tanaka faction, which, owing to the controversy of the Lockheed affair, has made his election impossible. In such cases the stronger faction will support one of the most suitable weaker factions.

2. After Tanaka had been ousted from the chair of Prime Minister on account of the Lockheed scandal, there were two possible successors, Ohira and Fukuda, who were of the same strength. However, both factions had come to a stalemate and Miki, whose faction was much smaller, was chosen. In 1976 Miki was ousted when all other factions, who believed his policies to be unfair, joined forces against him, and he was replaced by Fukuda.

Part III
The Japanese—An Agrarian People seen from the point of view of History

Part III

10 The Emperor as the Chief High Priest of Agrarian Ceremonies

A mountain of evidence suggests that Japan was, from the start, an agricultural country.

Through the Ise Shrine and the Emperor, many rituals have continued from prehistoric times thousands of years ago up to the present day, and they may hardly seem appropriate to a modern enlightened country. Although Japan is now best known for its high-technology goods the symbol of unity of the nation is an emperor who inherits unchanged agrarian ritual from prehistoric times. And that emperor symbolically carries out an agricultural cultivation even today, planting young rice-plants and reaping rice. The 'Don Peasant' spirit has been the unchanging spirit of the Japanese people since the 'age of the gods', and since the founding of the country.

If you were a Japanese in pre-war days, there were lines of verse called 'The Oracle' (Go-shinchoku) celebrating the occasion of 'The descent to earth of the grandson of the Sun Goddess' (Tenson Korin) which everyone learned by heart. These were the words spoken when the goddess Amaterasu sent her imperial grandson Prince Ninigi down to Japan. 'The land of fresh rice-ears of multiple harvests of the rich reed-plains, this is the land over which our descendants shall rule. I exhort you to govern it well and prosper. The prosperity of the Imperial throne shall last as long as heaven and earth.'

This evokes Japan as a country of ripening rice-plains, which must be governed by the descendants of the Imperial line and which is blest and endowed with unending prosperity. In this kind of folk memory, the ancestors of the Japanese were sent down from heaven in order to prosper in a rice-growing country.

The Emperor Jimmu (who was the first Emperor of the

115

early period) acceded to the throne, according to tradition, in the year 660 BC, in the oak-plain (Kashiwara) of Yamato. About the fourth year after the foundation by Jimmu, the record says 'standing in the festival garden of the mountain of Tomi, we vow obedience to our parents and praise the gods of heaven'. There was in this record the implication of the thanksgiving festival being for cereals, obedience to the oracle, diligent labour in the fields, and the production of wonderful cereal crops.

Had the Japanese been an equestrian people, or perhaps a pastoral people, a lamb rather than cereals would have been offered on a mountain top to the god of heaven. We cannot know exactly what this festival on Mount Tomi was, but since it has been traditionally described and celebrated for centuries up to the present time, as 'the Harvest Festival' (*Nii-name-no-matsuri, Nii-name-sai*) or 'the Great Harvest-offering Festival' (*Ō-Nie-no-Matsuri*), we can surmise its essential features.

The Harvest Festival is held on 23 November every year and in it the Emperor celebrates the provision of new rice through the action of Imperial ancestors from the time of the Emperor Jimmu, and the gods of heaven and earth, and the myriad deities. It is, moreover, a festival when he himself eats certain foods. The festival acquires a special significance when it is carried out by a newly enthroned emperor for the first time. This originates in Emperor Jimmu's festival at Mount Tomi in 656 BC.

In this festival the Emperor, together with all the spirits of his imperial ancestors and all the gods, determines by tortoise-shell divination, in which the shell is used as an indicator, two places in different fields for the sowing of seeds of rice which are to be eaten. This is called 'fixing the points of the fields of food' (*Saiden-tentei*) and the fields are called respectively *Yuki* field and *Suki* field. The owners of these fields thus 'fixed' cultivate them by sowing seeds after purifying their bodies. The heads of the rice thus produced are treated solemnly as the incarnation of the goddess of harvest, Toyo-uke, who is celebrated in the Outer Shrine at Ise. After a ceremony to dedicate the new cereal at the Daijo Shrine (where there is a *Yuki* Hall and a *Suki* Hall), the new Emperor eats the new cereal with his imperial ancestor Sun Goddess Amaterasu Ōmikami. This two-fold ceremony is carried out when a new Emperor accedes to the Throne. The 'accession to the throne' is metaphysical and ceremonial and is known as 'the Accession to the Heavenly Imperial Throne of the Sun' showing the new Emperor as authentic descendant of Amaterasu Ōmikami, the imperial ancestor who is identified with the sun goddess. The other great harvest offering, Ō-Nie festival, unlike the accession ceremony itself, which is directed to heaven, is more earthbound, for the Ō-Nie festival is an agrarian ritual derived from the 'blessing of the rice-ear of the food garden'. The imperial ancestor, the goddess Amaterasu Ōmikami, gave a rice-ear to the heavenly Prince Ninigi who descended to Japan; it had been planted in Takama-ga-hara (the heavenly plain) and Japan was supposed to prosper when it was cultivated. The words written in Nihon Shoki; 'I bequeath to my imperial son the rice-ear of the garden in Takama-ga-hara'—is a command to the imperial grandson to produce rice.

There are two main theories about the origin of the word *ine* ('rice-ear'). One is 'ii-no-ne' ('root of rice') and 'i-no-ne' ('root of life') where 'i' stands for 'inochi' ('life'). However, because probably the root word 'ii' ('rice') is also the word 'i' ('spirit') which saves life, or the word 'i', (standing for 'breach', 'iki'), then 'ine' ('rice-ear') means 'the root of life', and should be seen as the interpretation adopted by the Japanese of ancient times. This rice-ear is considered to be the incarnation of the sacred being Toyo-uke, the granddaughter of the god who sprang from the urine of Izanami-no-mikoto, the female creator of the islands of Japan.

The fact that the new Emperor eats this rice-ear with Amaterasu Ōmikami (that is to say, at the shrine, before the goddess) at the Ō-Nie Festival ('Great Food Offering Festival') shows it to be a ritual in which the Emperor physically inherits the country, Japan.

THE BIRTH OF A TRADITION IN WHICH DIFFERENT RELIGIONS CO-EXIST

I have mentioned before that the concepts of an agrarian society are succinctly expressed in Article No. 1 of Prince

Shōtoku's constitution (604): 'Respect harmony'. This view can be seen nowhere more clearly than in the way the two religions of Shinto and Buddhism have been able to co-exist in Japan.

When Buddhism entered Japan for the first time, things did not go entirely smoothly. When a statue of the Buddha was sent to the Emperor Kin-Mei (d. 571) from Kudara (Korea), he was overcome by the solemnity and dignity which seemed to shine forth from it and summoned his court officials to discuss whether they should accept this faith. Iname of the Soga family and some others approved the idea of worshipping the image of the Buddha, since they inclined towards an international way of thinking; on the other hand, the old noble families of the Mononobes and Nakatomis vigorously opposed the worship of a god from another country, whereupon the Emperor Kin-Mei gave up the idea of conversion to Buddhism. The struggle between the Sogas on the one hand and the Mononobes and the Nakatomis on the other continued for a long time and it was not unheard of for statues of the Buddha to be found destroyed or thrown into ditches by those opposed to the religion. After many ups-and-downs, the Sogas were eventually victorious and the *Nihon Shoki* (Chapters 19 and 21) gives many details on the conversion to Buddhism of the Emperor Yomei (d. 587).

Yet Japan never became a truly Buddhist country. The authority of the great shrines which had survived from ancient times was maintained; also the Ise Shrine and the imperial accession ceremony and the harvest festival remained as before. At the same time, however, Buddhist temples were going up all over Japan and there were fervent Buddhist believers among both Emperors and Empresses.

For instance, the Emperor Tenmu (d. 636) was a fervent devotee of Buddhism and strictly forbade the taking of animal life; he searched throughout Japan until he had a complete collection of the Buddhist scriptures and was the first to have lectures given all over the country on the Konkōmyō Kyō (Suvarnaprabhâsa). When his Empress fell ill, he commanded work to begin on the building of the Yakushiji Temple which remains to this day famous for its architecture and sculpture. It was this Emperor, too, who ordered every household in the land to have a Buddhist image to worship. Yet it was, on the other hand, this very same Emperor who set up the system called *Shikinen sengū*, or 'shrine removal ceremony' by which the Ise Shrine is completely rebuilt on an adjoining site every 20 years and to which the objects of worship are transferred. This practise continues to this day.

Tenmu's readiness to pursue the new religion of Buddhism is often reflected in more recent times in people's enthusiasm in adopting new faiths of various kinds even to the point of abandoning their shelf of Shinto deities and the Buddhist altar which are normally kept in the home. However, in such cases, they may lose the respect of their neighbours because they have ceased to venerate their ancestors. In fact, religious fanaticism of any kind is regarded with suspicion in Japan, where visits to the Shinto or Buddhist centres of worship are reserved for such occasions as the New Year Festival or other national religious festivals. The notion that those who make too frequent pilgrimages to temples or shrines were light women, gamblers, robbers and people of their ilk, still remains.

THE ORIGIN IN ANCIENT JAPAN OF REVERENCE FOR HARMONY MORE THAN FOR RELIGION

In that sense, the family mottoes of Kobayakawa Takakage (d. 1597), the famous general of the Civil War period, is characteristically Japanese: 'Shaka's creed has its points, so long as we don't forget reason'. By 'Shaka's creed', of course, he meant Buddhism, but I think we should extend the phrase to mean broadly 'religion' in general. The value of reading religious books and having faith should not outweigh reason, the way of the ordinary world. We tend to put the teachings of religion in one pan of the balance and the reason of the world should weigh rather more heavily.

Precisely because the Emperor Tenmu *was* Emperor, the co-existence of the two religions seems to have come about throughout Japan from above. However, even if that is how it was, it was not a forced procedure. Since you could not

very well live in a peaceful agrarian society, like that of
Japan, by ostentatiously practising a religion which easily
becomes an absolute, the tacit recognition of the principle
of 'harmony' as superior to that of religion must have been
natural among the common people.

The Emperor Tenmu and Prince Shōtoku are the summit
of the structure. As an example of the bottom end, let us
quote once more *The Mad Village*.

> The mutually hostile Buddhist sects, the Shin sect and
> Zen, co-exist peacefully in the village. Not only do the
> followers of Zen, who believe in the doctrine of
> justification by works and self-reliance, attend the prayers
> of the Shin Sect, whose followers believe in salvation by
> faith, and rely on the benevolence of Amida Buddha, but
> no one finds it strange that the Zen believers themselves
> have prayer gatherings.
>
> There is something all-embracing in the harmony and
> life of the village, and it seems to permit the co-existence
> of mutually hostile elements.[1]

Over and above this, there is the Shinto shrine. Differences of religion, differences of sect, are of no value when it
comes to disturbing the harmony of the village. 'How very
convenient!', foreigners are bound to think wryly when they
observe Japan putting the solidarity of country and village
above religion and sects. They naturally wonder whether
the Japanese can think accurately or are unaware of the
laws of contradiction when they can allow two or three
religions to co-exist in their minds. Yet, in a sense, Japan is
more advanced than they.

In Western Europe the religious reformation which began
in the 16th century reached a tragic extreme with the
Thirty Years War (1618–48) in the first half of the 17th
century, a war deeply related to religious issues, in which
Germany was the main theatre. When men reflected on
what had happened, they came to the broad recognition
that it was stupid to go to war as a result of making
sectarian religion the highest value, and that perhaps different religions *could* co-exist within a single state. In other
words, you respect the harmony of the nation more than
the value of your religion. The question whether the state

itself should take precedence over the religions within the state lay at the very heart of the Enlightenment. Frederick the Great (1712–86), enlightened despot, made Prussia great and strong by employing able persons in the service of the state without asking questions about their religious beliefs. The modern state acquired great strength once the ideas of the Enlightenment were confirmed as its principle.

Great Britain is the best example of this. Under the Union Jack, both Anglicans and Non-conformists fought hard for their country.

CODIFYING THE PRINCIPLE OF HARMONY: PRINCE SHŌTOKU (d. 622)

Japan experienced her own Enlightenment a long, long time ago. It began with Prince Shōtoku who promulgated the decree of the furtherance of the Three Treasures,[2] that is, the furtherance of Buddhism, in the second year of the reign of the Empress Suiko (594 AD). He also ensured that the local gods were worshipped throughout Japan by a decree promulgated five years later (599 AD). There had been a great earthquake in April of that year, many houses and temples were destroyed, and men wondered if the gods of Japan were angry.

The land of Japan had been established by the two gods Izanagi (male) and Izanami (female), and there must have been a fair number of people who thought it impossible to worship strange gods (Buddhist images) in Japan with impunity.

The 'edict of piety'—'revering the gods'—was promulgated on 29 February of the 15th year of the Empress Suiko (607 AD). At the head of a hundred court officials, the Empress, with Prince Shōtoku and the Minister Soga-no-Umako, prayed to the gods of Japan. Yet in the previous years two images of the Buddha had been made, 16 feet high, one of copper and one of brocade, and the copper one had been deposited in the Golden Hall of the Gankō Temple. It was decided that every year, from that year on, on 8 April and 15 July, ceremonies would be carried out at every temple. This was the beginning of Kanbutsu-e (the celebration of the anniversary of Buddha's birth) and Urabon (the Feast of Lanterns, a Buddhist counterpart to All Souls' Day).

In July of that year, also, Prince Shōtoku lectured on the Sōmani Sutra and the Lotus Sutra at the Okamoto Palace. This was very pleasing to the Empress Suiko. We get the impression that the whole Imperial Family was infatuated with the new religion, Buddhism. In the following year this same Empress promulgated the 'decree of piety (revering the gods)' and she and the Prince, accompanied by a hundred court officials, made visits to Shinto shrines. This is the important thing to remember, that the Empress who began the celebration of the anniversary of Buddha's birth and the Feast of Lanterns was the same who, at about the same time, ordered that the Shinto gods of ancient times should be worshipped.

We must also remember that the Seventeen-clause Constitution of Prince Shōtoku was issued about this time (12th year of the Empress Suiko; 604 AD). That period in history, the beginning of the 7th century, must be remembered as the time when Japan's 'principle of harmony' was codified. In fact, we may consider it as Japan's 'Year One of the Enlightenment'. And that Seventeen-clause Constitution itself clearly demonstrated the ideas of an agrarian society.

THE PRECEPTS OF THE 'DON PEASANT' SPIRIT AS SEEN IN THE SEVENTEEN-CLAUSE CONSTITUTION

The significance of the first clause of Prince Shōtoku's constitution, 'Respect harmony', is further enhanced when we realise the phrase is that of a man who commissioned Buddhist images and also visited Shinto shrines to pay due homage officially, for the sake of harmony. In honouring harmony, the necessity of avoiding feelings of envy caused by any form of superiority arises. This is dealt with precisely in the 14th clause. He says:

In the fourteenth place the body of ministers, the hundred officials, should not have spite or envy. If we envy other men, other men will envy us too. Evil derived from envy knows no end; thus people tend not to rejoice in superior wisdom; if you have surpassing talent you will be the object of envy.

Prince Shōtoku must have said this time and time again. The Prince continues. Let us interpret what he says:

If we continue to envy men who have greater talent and wisdom than ourselves in this way, we may produce a single wise man every five hundred years, but no holy man will emerge even every thousand years. If wise men emerge rarely, and holy men emerge never—how shall we govern the country properly?

He knew the danger of the envy-society; it is difficult to produce men of wisdom and goodness on which those who govern a country can model themselves; when eagles with ability keep their claws hidden, society will slip backwards as long as those claws are concealed.

In the 10th clause Prince Shōtoku has indicated that in an agrarian society such as that of Japan it is impossible to dictate to people by exercising powerful leadership. In the village assent must be sought by discussions with everybody. When Japan is at peace there is no need for the top men to decide important matters quickly. In fact it is harmful. 'The common man' means 'everybody'. 'All men are average men' affirmed Prince Shōtoku. It is remarkable in the development of egalitarianism that a prince, ranking next to the Emperor (in his case the Empress) proclaimed this in the 10th clause of his Constitution as early as the first part of 604 AD. Let us summarise the intention of Clause 10:

Men should not allow themselves to be roused to anger. Men should not show anger in their faces. Every man in his heart is convinced that he is right. If the opportunity is good for your opponent, it is bad for you. If it is good for you, it is bad for him. You yourself are not always a saint and your opponent is not invariably a fool. *You and he are both only ordinary men.* Whoever he be, none can determine the rights and wrongs of a thing. Your oppo-

nent and you are both wise and foolish. Even though you
are under the impression that you alone know what is
right, remember to behave as if everyone else was similarly
convinced about himself.

This is probably the first record in which the collectivism of
the Japanese is advocated. They are the words of a real
village sage. If everyone in the village is equal and has the
same rights, each must bear the others in mind. If you have
faith in yourself, remember that your neighbour also has
faith in himself. It is mutual, so when we act, let us all co-
operate together; and that is what happens.

So a leader's arbitrary actions are unacceptable. Hence
the phrasing of the last clause of the constitution, which is
still alive in the Liberal Democratic Party, in the country
village, in the bureaucracy, in society, in our schools: 'In the
17th place, you must never decide great matters on your
own. You must always discuss them with all kinds of people'.

NOTES

1.   Kida Minoru, op. cit., p. 52.
2.   The Three Treasures, namely Buddha, his laws and the priests.

11 The Civil War Period and the Foresight of Tokugawa Ieyasu, the First of the Tokugawa Shōguns

THE RETURN TO THE AGRARIAN CONCEPT—THE HEIAN PERIOD (794–1192) AND THE KAMAKURA PERIOD (1192–1333); BOTH FUNCTION ACCORDING TO THE AGRARIAN PRINCIPLE

The new Emperor of the Heian Period (794–1192) acceded to the throne by the accession ceremony and the O-Nie-no-Matsuri (the Great Food Offering Festival). Since an emperor whose accession ceremony was performed but who had not been able to carry out the O-Nie-no-Matsuri was called 'Han Tei' (Half-Emperor), we realise that the Emperor's role as the high priest of the agriculture festival was unchanged.

The Heian aristocracy was a narrow society, centred on the Fujiwara clan. The Fujiwara clan were a courtier family that wielded great political power during the Heian period. So complete was its power over the Imperial Court during the period of regency government, and so pervasive was its influence on the culture of that time that the years between 850 to 1166 are often referred to as the Fujiwara period. Everybody knew everybody else, and it was known that if you traced back your genealogy, you would be related to everyone else. This corresponds exactly to the agrarian notion, 'neighbours never change'.

One of the characteristics of the Heian period is said to have been that the death penalty was never meted out for political crime. It is amazing in view of the way the world is now that for many centuries such a thing was possible. For example, Sugawara-no-Michizane who counselled both emperors Uda and Daigo and posed a serious threat to Fujiwara rule was merely exiled to Kyushu. This was considered such a great tragedy that men of that time were scared of his vengeful spirit after his death. But Michizane was in fact allocated the rank of Dazai-Gon-no-Sotsu (deputy viceroy of southern Japan). He was not punished by death, nor by total exile. The Dazai-Fu office (A garrison city near Fukuoka City in Kyushu) controlled Kyushu, Iki and Tsushima islands which were Japan's back-door at that time, a strategically important spot in terms of diplomacy and national defence. But for a man who had exercised the functions of Minister of the Right, to be deputy Commander-in-Chief at that spot was a fairly harsh relegation; nevertheless, since in contemporary terms his crime was the crime of treason, the punishment was a moderate one.

What we call the 'court of the Heian period' should be termed 'the Fujiwara village'. Michizane felt that he had been ostracised from that village. Ostracism inflicts a dreadful anguish on a human being but it is not capital punishment.

The period of the military castes (buke) which followed the Heian period, differs from it, in rigorously imposing the law, and gives the impression of a return to the pre-Heian period.

The origins of the samurai (military castes) lay in the agricultural classes who worshipped both the Shinto kami and the Buddha. They were men of powerful provincial families to start with, and they achieved power while discharging the duty of maintaining the peace in Kyoto. However, in the beginning their status was low and the admission to the Imperial Court of Hachimantaro Yoshiie, who was of the powerful Minamoto clan and subdued Mutsu (in the northeastern part of the Main Island), only took place in the second year of Shōtoku (1098).

Despite being military adventurers always on the move, the samurai way of thinking was still that of an agrarian society. The samurai were the combat group of an agrarian society. Of course, those who showed ability in battle in the Minamoto and Taira periods received 'rewards' but there was no feeling of 'selection'. There was no awareness of difference of ability between a general and his subordinates: simply, the vassals served their lord. Even if he had less ability than they had, the lord was the lord. That was his hereditary 'standing' (*mibun*).

THE JŌEI CODE TRANSMITS THE SPIRIT OF PRINCE SHŌTOKU

When the Hōjō Shogunate succeeded the Minamoto Shogunate its fundamental character did not change. In the first year of Jōei (1232),[1] at the time of Hōjō Yasutoki (d. 1242), were drawn up the 51 articles of the Goseibai Code (the Jōei Code) which must be considered the basis of *samurai* law. They codified usages which had arisen naturally, from ancient times, between the manor and its *samurai*. If we may borrow Yasutoki's own expression, he put in writing 'the customs of the *samurai* and the rules of the people'. It is customary law, codified in 51 articles, three times as many as the Seventeen-Clause Constitution of Prince Shōtoku and vastly different from the ancient Codes of Laws (671, 701, 718) with more than one thousand articles. However, contrary to the ancient Codes of Laws which had in many cases no great impact on men in general and were promulgated only nominally, this code of Yasutoki sprang up naturally between manor and *samurai* in the very earliest times. Because it gave indications of what would be accepted as the 'reasonableness' of the *samurai*, based on the judicial precedents of Yoritomo, the founder of the shogunate, its practical effectiveness was great and it filtered quite naturally right down to the bottom layers of society. It was more than a mere nominal code; and even after the Hōjō Shogunate disappeared, the code was respected as the customary law of the *samurai*. The gist of this *samurai* law lay in demonstrating in writing, on a national basis, how to try civil litigation concerning disputes over land.

As *samurai* were originally farmers, boundary disputes over land were a real problem. There was nothing at all in the Taihō Code of Laws (701) to help solve them, nor in the Yōrō Code of Laws (718) which imitated the Laws of T'ang

China. There had to be something in which 'reasonableness' was founded on custom. That alone could win the approval of men who clung to their land as the only spot on the soil of Japan where they lived out their whole lives. And behind that 'reasonableness' it is impossible to be unaware of the feelings of an agrarian society. For example, the authority of parents to dispose of land is absolute. Land is 'privately owned'. The choice of how to divide it among the children remains the parents' prerogative; that is the principle. In particular, when private landowners have carried out a conveyancing between themselves, the individual's document made up on that occasion has greater force than the *ando-jō*, which is the document of assurance of the shogunate, the public document which acknowledges the ownership of land.

The private ownership of land was absolute and it is striking how much more important it was than the shogunate's documents.

In common with all countries today, modern Japan has a land expropriation law, but it is extremely difficult to activate. Even when major highways are being constructed within Tokyo City, the work may come to a halt for long periods because one or two small houses cannot be demolished. This is the Don Peasant attitude manifesting itself, showing its firm hold on the private ownership of land, so firm that even the Kamakura Shogunate found it necessary to avoid interfering with it.

Another essential agrarian component of the Jōei Code is its respect for women's rights. When the code says 'a parent', father and mother are treated alike, without distinction. It may be true that the ancient codes of laws in Japan were an imitation of the T'ang system; nevertheless, the Japanese codes did recognise women's rights.

For instance, in the T'ang laws, as long as there was a man capable of inheriting, the wife or other woman had no right of inheritance at all, but in the Yōrō Code of Laws (718) there was something approximating to equal rights for man and woman, in the matter of succession. The *samurai* code also inherited this spirit, and women as well as men could be private owners of a fief. The woman could offer a man as her deputy when she seemed incapable of fulfilling the fief's duty to the shogunate. The disinheritance of a woman's warrior fief occurred later because, in the great confusion of a country torn by war, a *samurai* society measured everything by the yardstick of strength in battle.

It was not always so. Because the woman was as important as the man in an agrarian society, the custom of recognising a woman's right of inheritance persisted (in an old-fashioned agrarian society like that of Japan), even into the *samurai* code.

'PUNISH BOTH SIDES IN A QUARREL': THE COMPLETE CONTRAST TO THE SPIRIT OF LAW

Punishing both sides in a quarrel, as might be expected, was not made explicit in the Jōei Code (1232); it arose quite naturally as a method of solving disputes over land and it was gradually but firmly settled as customary law.

When a dispute breaks out, it is quite outrageous—from the point of view of justice—to punish both sides without querying which side is in the right. But in real problems involving land disputes and so on, each side has its own case and no simple decision is possible. If the parties go to law, the case may be long and drawn out and even when it is heard with great goodwill on both sides, the defeated party may not acknowledge defeat. Moreover, in land disputes, because the concern is with boundaries, a case may very well not reach a complete settlement. So gradually 'harmony' rather that justice becomes the optimum value, and in the conviction that 'at any rate a fight does no one any good', we often decide to dispose of the problem as tidily as we can. And this has turned out to be the most efficient method.

In more mobile societies that are less concerned with such issues as boundaries, this type of justice would have no meaning and would belie the authority of a leader responsible for supervising trials based on a justice that is visible to all.

When young brothers in a family quarrel, the parent will not decide the case by enquiring who is right and who is wrong but will say, 'You're making a nuisance of yourselves! Patch it up, both of you!' And he usually exerts his authority by giving both the elder and the younger brother a good clout on the head. This is a punishment for being *involved* in the quarrel, because it is important that there be peace in the household. And this was an equally effective way of keeping the peace in a society of samurai who were quick to quarrel, following the principle that both parties to a quarrel should be punished, in complete contradiction to 'the spirit of the law'.

Religion offers another conspicuous example which shows how Japanese the Jōei Code is. Its first article is a command to 'revere the gods of Shinto and to maintain the shrines' and the second is a command 'to revere the Buddha and to maintain the temples'. It is quite clearly laid down: 'shrines and temples may be different but they are both to be accorded the same reverence.' The tradition of Prince Shōtoku, who valued harmony more than religion, is shown even more explicitly. I have pointed out before that the spirit which values harmony above religious sectarianism is the essence of the thought of the Enlightenment in 17th-century Europe, and the Kamakura Shogunate firmly adopted the policy shown by this Enlightenment principle in the 13th century. In Western terms, Hōjō Yasutoki, who established the Jōei Code, would probably qualify as an 'enlightened despot'.

A HETEROGENEOUS AGE IN JAPAN—THE WARRIOR CHIEFS OF THE CIVIL WAR PERIOD ANIMATED BY EQUESTRIAN PRINCIPLES.

Japan's long history as an agrarian society has not been uninterrupted. There have been exceptions, when an equestrian ethos prevailed. At various times in the past this distinctive tendency has manifested itself, such as during the Civil War period of 1467–1585 when ability was valued more highly than principles of harmony. The Meiji Restoration and the period after 1945 are also exceptions in this sense.

A different facet of the same ethos, more related to the internal structure of Japan than to a specific period in time, is the genesis of 'commerce'. In any kind of agrarian society, once you reach a certain degree of population level and cultural standards, commerce arises of its own accord. In commerce, profit and loss go hand in hand, and businesses prosper through an individual's power of judgement. They may also go bankrupt. The principle operating in this case is not agrarian but equestrian, and the problem is, how can it function in an agrarian society?

Let us first consider the Civil War period, which was an exceptional equestrian period in the history of Japan, and see if we can find in it a characteristically Japanese pattern.

What kind of a period was it? The answer must be, 'one in which Toyotomi Hideyoshi (1598)[2] was possible'.

There is no doubt that Hideyoshi is an outstanding hero in Japanese history. But had Hideyoshi not been born when he was, he would never have risen to power. Had he been born in the period of Prince Shōtoku, had he been born in the period of Yoritomo, or in the period of the Northern and Southern Dynasties, he could never have risen to the top. Still less, if he had been born in the Genroku era (1688–1703) or the Bunaka-Bunsei period (1804–29) of the Tokugawa Shogunate. Whatever good fortune he may have had, in those days he would probably have risen to be something like a Shogun's personal steward, or a rural boss in his native district of Owari; nothing more.

Even as far back as Prince Shōtoku (d. 622), if you did not belong to a great clan, you had no chance. Yoritomo (d. 1199) came to power because he was especially respected, from childhood, as the legitimate son of the Minamoto clan. And that Minamoto clan, too, had a remote lineage linking it with the Imperial House from the start. In the Nine Years' Campaign (1051–62) Minamoto Yoriyoshi consolidated the basis of the Minamoto clan by fearful battles in the northeastern part of the main island which occupied nearly a decade. Later, Minamoto Yoshiie, during the Three Years' Campaign (1083–87), in collaboration with his younger brother Yoshimitsu and others, destroyed the Kiyohara clan, subdued the Mutsu (in the northeastern part of the main island) and made the Minamoto clan the unshakable leader of the *samurai* groups. After Yoshiie (d. 1106) had become revered as the first *samurai* to be granted the privilege of attending the Imperial Court within the Hall in 1098, a further hundred years had to pass before his descendant of direct lineage known as the 'barbarian-subduing marshal', founded the Kamakura Shogunate in 1192.

So, although the *samurai* were an ability-based group, their success was not as rapid as it would have been in an equestrian society, because they had evolved in the first place from an agrarian society. The combination of lord and retainer, with lords granting favour to *samurai* groups subordinated to them from generation to generation, ensured finally that the leader of the Minamoto clan would be the founder of the shogunate. Hideyoshi's case was very different. To have moved to the top in one generation had been inconceivable before him.

But in the Civil War period (1467–1585) that was possible. The Hōjō family of Kantō, the Saito family of Mino and so on were all men of humble origins who availed themselves of the opportunity of extraordinary times and became feudal lords, even if they did not achieve as much as Hideyoshi. Even though Nobunaga (d. 1582) and Ieyasu (d. 1616) were more elevated than Hideyoshi in their origins, they were still only children of petty lords of provincial fiefs. Their acquisition of power by ability and nothing else is characteristic of the Civil War period. It is from that time, too, that historical narratives and popular novels begin to be interesting.

THE SPEED OF HIDEYOSHI'S ACQUISITION OF POWER, A RESULT OF THE 'FAIRNESS' OF AN EQUESTRIAN SOCIETY

The example of Takeda Shingen (d. 1573) shows how much ability was respected in the Civil War period. Shingen became the head of the house of Takeda by banishing his father Takeda Nobutora. More striking than the event itself is the continued admiration for and devotion to Shingen on the part of his retainers and the people of the Takeda domain afterwards.

The cause of this admiration was no doubt Shingen's character, but there is also the prime fact that he had not been beaten in battle. Shingen had fought tough battles with Uesugi Kenshin (d. 1578) at Kawa Nakajima but he was undefeated and his domain was greatly extended. There is nothing worse than being in service to a lord who is defeated in battle. If your lord wins, his fief increases and your probability of survival increases likewise. What the people of a fief feared most was to see their own fields turned into battlefields and their houses burned to the ground. Shingen's battlefields were all outside his own domain, and he always won. And when he committed the crime of banishing his father, everyone looked the other way.

This logic generally prevailed in the Civil War period. If the lord was incapable, his retainers died in battle and the fief houses were burned in the fires of war. If the elder brother was weak, he was removed to a temple and a stronger younger brother became the lord. If the elder brother refused to be persuaded, there were other ways—dose of poison perhaps. And daughters were ruthlessly used as pawns in strategic marriages for the security of the fief. Sons were made hostages. Anything and everything was done to ensure the security of the lord and his group of retainers.

Neighbouring lands were not constant, nor were boundaries, domains were forever changing. A war with neighbouring domains could break out at any time. When such a state continued for a hundred years, opinions and customs changed. The right of women to inherit a domain became out of the question. Oda Nobunaga[3] shows most admirably these changing customs and attitudes to life. Hideyoshi profited from them. He rapidly promoted pages chosen from villages in his native province to the rank of *daimyō* (feudal lord) with no question of enquiring about their birth and social position. And he showed a sentiment the English call 'fair play', when he guaranteed that those daimyō who surrendered to him should retain their fiefs. Although the Shimazu clan of Kyushu, the Mori clan of Chūgoku and the Chōsokabe clan of Shikoku were originally Hideyoshi's great enemies, they were instantly won round and came over to the side of Hideyoshi's son at the battle of Sekigahara. Hideyoshi's treatment of all the *daimyōs* who surrendered, compelled this respect since it certainly conformed to justice. Because this treatment was obvious to everyone, the unification of Japan went forward at a rapid pace. When Nobunaga was killed at Honnōji Temple, he was still some way from taking power. Hideyoshi was just one of his generals but in the following three years he became chief adviser to the Emperor (*Kanpaku*) and within five years he subdued the whole country from Kyushu to Ou and moved Ieyasu to Edo (now Tokyo) from his ancestral citadels Mikawa and Suruga.

Hideyoshi's rapid seizure of power was amazing. Here is the ability principle at work: real rewards and real punishments. By behaving fairly to those who had surrendered and doing away with road barriers to promote commerce and trade he was, basically, exactly like Genghis Khan. And the speed of his expedition was as fast as Genghis Khan's.

The Azuchi Momoyama period (1576–98) was, for Japan, a period of exceptionally active equestrian thought. Splendid buildings were constructed, like the castles of Azuchi, Osaka and Himeji. The same is true of paintings. Had the Hideyoshi period continued, and had the country not been closed to the outside world, then architecture, the fine arts and crafts on a grand scale would have been produced, creating a Japanese Renaissance.

Tokugawa Ieyasu[4] was a notable figure in the Civil War period but most striking is the fact that he was also responsible for bringing it to an end, and for consciously abandoning the way of thinking of people like Hideyoshi.

Ieyasu was born in the 11th year of Tenbun (1542), 75 years after the start of the Ōnin Wars (1467) which mark the beginning of the Civil War period; and he died in the second year of Genna (1616), at the age of 75. So Tokugawa Ieyasu was born in the very middle of the Civil War period and was the man who brought it to a close.

After the battle of Okehazama in Owari (1560) and the battle of Anegawa in Ōmi (1570) up to the battle of Sekigahara (1600) and the summer camp of Osaka (1615) few men had fought in more important engagements. And he took power by using his ability. Successful men usually respect the principles by which they themselves have succeeded. Men who have saved money by thrift respect thrift. Men who have made a name for themselves by hard work respect hard work. But Ieyasu was not that kind of man. In the *Bokusaiki* (Bokusai's biography of Ieyasu) there is the following account of him:

> From the time he was young, Lord Ieyasu grew up in the army camps and lived the roughest life on the battlefield, exposed to wind and rain, toil and hardships. He took part in battles without number, both great and small. Because of this he did not have leisure to read books and listen to discourses. He took power on horseback because he was exceedingly able, like a god in his nature, a man of great intellectual power. Because this was his character, he early understood that you cannot govern a country on horseback. As a result, he always revered and believed in the way of sages and governed the country and the state accordingly. For him there was no way other than to live and rule in accordance with the ultimate nature of humanity.

Here the idea 'take power on horseback, but do not govern on horseback' appears, in the terms used by a Confucian official to Liu Pang, the founder of the Han Dynasty in China: 'Your Majesty, even if we obtain power on horseback, should we also govern on horseback?'[5]

To take power on horseback, that is by using one's ability, is to take it in accordance with an equestrian concept. But if we try to preserve the power thus taken for any length of time, we should not attempt this by the same equestrian means. That was valid for ancient China which was basically agrarian, and Ieyasu understood this very clearly.

It appears from all accounts that Ieyasu studied Confucianism from the age of 52 (the second year of Bunroku, 1593). At this time Ieyasu invited to Edo Fujiwara Seika, who had a reputation as a scholar of the Sung School of Confucianism, and had him lecture on the *Jōgan-Seiyō*. That he chose this book as a text is profoundly significant. It is a collection of political discussions between the second Emperor (practically the founder) of the T'ang Dynasty and his wise retainers. The Emperor's reign was peaceful and prosperous, so that it is known in Japan as 'the Peaceful Era of Jōgan' (627–49). The Emperor was a wise ruler, rare in the history of China. So this book had become required reading for Chinese emperors, a classic to teach them the methods of rule over an empire.

Remember that the year in which Ieyasu began to study Confucian books of this type and have lectures given was the second year of Bunroku (December 1593).

In the previous year Hideyoshi had sent out his expedition to Korea. The Japanese Army won a great victory. Encouraged by the successful offensive of Konishi Yukinaga who had set out from Tsushima on 12 April, occupied Pusan the next day and on 2 May took Seoul, Hideyoshi decided to go ahead and attack the Ming also, and on 15 June Kuroda Nagamasa occupied Pyongyang. But when they took on the military might of the Ming, it was not in the least like fighting the Korean Army, either in numbers or equipment.

By April of the following year, the second year of Bunroku, they had to withdraw from Seoul and peace negotiations were started. They handed over the two princes of Korea who had been captured by Katō Kiyomasa. Then Hideyoshi moved out of the camp at Nagoya in Hizen (Kyūshū Island) and returned to Osaka. Ieyasu was in Nagoya and returned to Edo at the end of October. Two months later he issued the invitation to Fujiwara Seika, the most eminent scholar in Japan.

IEYASU'S FOUR CONDITIONS FOR PEACE

While he was in northern Kyushu, what was Ieyasu thinking about? Hideyoshi had taken power in Japan by military force—on horseback—and, not stopping at that, had sent his men on into Korea, and had even gone on to assault the Ming. Did Ieyasu not see the foolishness of this? If you have taken power on horseback, there may well be no end to war. After taking power, it is best to cease acting as if you were still on horseback. He may have realised this.

Two months after returning to Edo he organised lectures

on the *Jōgan Seiyō* and they seem to have been a great success. For more than 20 years afterwards he devoted himself to endless study and learned that it was necessary to use enlightened methods in exercising the power he had obtained on horseback. He drew up a definite plan which involved abandoning the equestrian concept. Nothing was so harmful to the peace of a country and the state as the ability principle. Perpetual peace was founded on a structure in which ability was completely blocked and could not be used. Ieyasu made this the basic plan of the shogunate which was nothing more or less than a return to agrarian concepts.

Ieyasu made a number of decisions to this end but the foundations of the 300 years' peace of the Tokugawa lie in the following four points.

First, the system of strict primogeniture. However much human beings strive, no one can overtake an elder brother in terms of age. There is no gap by which ability can penetrate. The younger brothers easily become reconciled to the inheritance. If the inheritance were to go to the ablest and most outstanding man, envy and contention would arise along with the intrigues which accompany them, and the group of retainers would be divided among themselves. But if you have primogeniture, independent of the dullness or wisdom of the eldest son, the seeds of dispute do not exist. If you live in a permanently peaceful country, then, the tranquillity of the household is preserved even if the eldest son is a blockhead. Disturbing the 'harmony' of the house, causing an uproar in the domestic scene, would be the only risk. The establishment of primogeniture is the most effective method of preventing it.

In the second place, the policy of the Tokugawa was to follow precedent, unless official notices were issued in special cases. Even when trials took place over boundary disputes about land, 'justice' was not the issue. What was in the old documents was what counted. If you can say, 'This is how it was from ancient times,' discussions and disputes on who is right and who is wrong are difficult to pursue. And as a principle, the villages of every region governed themselves according to the customs of former times.

Thirdly, women were not involved at all in inheritance

and public office. In the beginning the Kamakura Shogunate recognised that women could inherit a domain, but this gradually fell into disuse: the seeds of dispute grew, for example, because of the death of a married woman with a domain as dowry, and too many unpleasant and insoluble problems resulted.

Fourthly, the fixing of classes and the division into warrior, peasant, artisan and merchant. This fixed a man in the class into which he was born and had no connection with his aptitudes or suitability.

If we look at the above four points, what·they have in common is a realisation of how a man may be reconciled to his condition. If his condition is made to depend on his ability, the result is endless conflict. If our status is fixed for ever at birth, it is easy to be reconciled to it. People who were unable to inherit the patrimony of a *daimyō*—'because I had an elder brother', 'because I am a woman', 'because I was born a tradesman'—were apparently resigned to it. Anyway, because their condition had no connection with their efforts or their ability, there was literally 'nothing to be done'. Apart from the hardening into fixed classes, in the fourth point, there seemed to be no dissatisfaction over the other three right to the end of the shogunate (1867). As far as inheritance was concerned, the civil code under the Meiji constitution (1889) was like the Tokugawa Code, and almost every household, we might say, was content.

IEYASU'S REAL INTENTION IN MAKING PRIMOGENITURE ABSOLUTE

So the first point, the system of primogeniture, seems to be particularly important. The second generation Shogun, Hidetada, had four sons. The eldest son Chōmaru died early and three sons were left: the second son Takechiyo (later the third Shogun Iemitsu), the third son Kunimatsumaro (later known as Suruga Chief Councillor Tadanaga) and the fourth son Yukimatsumaro (later known as Hoshina Masayuki).

The last son was not born of a legal wife so the issue in

his case is different. The problem lay between Iemitsu and Tadanaga. Since the younger brother, Kunimatsumaro (Tadanaga), had been extraordinarily intelligent from an early age, his mother, that is, Hidetada's wife, doted on him specially. Influenced by his wife, Hidetada himself seems to have had a strong affection for the younger son. As both the Shogun and his wife held him in such great affection, the family retainers did likewise. And the rumour was secretly whispered abroad that it looked as if the younger brother were going to be the third Shogun. Ofuku (later called Kasuga-no-tsubome), the wet nurse of the elder brother Takechiyo (Iemitsu), was distressed at this. If the younger brother were to inherit power, a long series of power struggles would ensue. She complained of this to Ieyasu, who was in retirement in Sumpu, through the intervention of Okaji, Ieyasu's favourite concubine. 'This is merely Ofuku being jealous', said Ieyasu, and took no notice. Whereupon Ofuku let it be known that she was making a pilgrimage to the Ise Shrine, passed through Sumpu, had an audience with Ieyasu, and gave him a detailed account of what was happening.

Ieyasu listened to the facts and was amazed at how the matter had grown in importance. If a dispute should arise between the two brothers over who should become Shogun, the country would immediately be plunged again in the civil war conditions of Genki (1570–73) and Tenshō (1573–91). So, in October, in the first year of Genna (1615), 'I want to go hawking', said Ieyasu, 'in the Kantō Plain', and suddenly took off for Edo. The Shogun Hidetada went out to meet him as far as Kanagawa and his two grandsons Takechiyo and Kunimatsumaro greeted him in Edo. A confrontation took place in Edo Castle, at the Western Outworks.

Ieyasu took Takechiyo (Iemitsu) by the hand, and set him in the upper seat. The ever-beloved younger brother Kunimatsumaro (Tadanaga) went along with his brother thinking it to be perfectly natural. 'Takechiyo is the man who will become lord, as the future Shogun', said Ieyasu, turning the younger brother back, 'and you are his retainer. You cannot sit in the same place.'

Next they went in to dine. Ieyasu ate with Takechiyo and Kunimatsumaro went to a lower seat and had to eat there.

As Ieyasu had made a distinction in this way, beyond the shadow of a doubt, between elder and younger brother, Kunimatsumaro and Hidetada themselves, and Hedetada's wife who bore him a special love, and their retainers, were thunderstruck. They turned pale. It had been made quite clear, before everyone, that it was impossible for the younger brother to become shogun by setting aside the elder. The younger brother had been surrounded by retainers who toadied to him, thinking he was going to be the third shogun, but now such rumours and speculations were completely stamped out and it was made as clear as day to them who the third shogun was going to be.

THE COUNTRY PROSPERS WHEN 'THE FIRST BORN IS A DUNCE': THE EVIDENCE OF HISTORY

A similar question arose at the time of Yoshimune, the eighth shogun (d. 1751). His eldest son, Chōfukumaru (later the ninth Shogun, Ieshige), was a very sick man, and an imbecile to boot, but the next son, Kojirō (later Tayasu Munetake) was a first-rate man. He was a cultured person, fond of Japanese literature, and had studied under Kada-no-Arimaro and Kamo-no-Mabuchi. He would have made an excellent head of the shogunal family, and there are poems by him, critical works on literature, poetics, *gagaku*—ancient court music—and ancient court usages. He was well versed in military skills, too, and was said to be a first-class archer. In comparison with the elder brother, his superiority is painfully obvious: on the one hand an imbecile intelligence inside a sickly body, on the other hand a man regarded as a second Ieyasu, accomplished both as artist and soldier.

If the Civil War period had been one in which ability spoke for itself, the younger brother should have succeeded to the shogunate without more ado. However, Yoshimune knew perfectly well what Ieyasu's command meant. If the decision were taken to fix the shogunate according to the wisdom or stupidity of the heir, there would be massive upheaval in the shogun's household, involving not only the shogun's family but also the *daimyōs*, the lesser lords, the flag-bearers and the retainers; and, following that, a great upheaval in the country at large. He saw that. He did not hesitate. As Ninth Shogun he appointed Ieshige, the sickly, weak imbecile, and employed the intelligent younger brother elsewhere.

It was common knowledge that Ieshige was an imbecile who could not speak even Japanese well and needed Ōoka Izumonokami, his knight-in-waiting, to interpret what he said. But the people of those days understood perfectly well that he mattered, because he had succeeded to the headship of the family; he was the eldest son.

Interestingly enough, the period of Shogun Ieshige was not at all a bad time for Japan. In the field of drama, Takeda Izumo's representative plays such as *Kanadehon Chūshingura* and *Sugawara Denju Tenarai Kagami* were written, and the famous actor Sawamura Sōjūrō was active in the theatre. In national literature, we have the names of Kamo-no-Mabuchi, the philologist, and Yanagizawa Kien, the *daimyō* scholar, and in Sino-Japanese poetry that of the famous Chinese scholar, Hattori Nankaku.

People in general could not have been unhappy in an epoch when such a popular drama as *Chūshingura* was written. The Shogun Ieshige was the perfect example of the phrase 'eldest son, least clever', but when society under his rule flourished, we could say 'eldest son, least clever, but we can cope' or even 'eldest son, least clever, that's the best way of all'.

This way of thinking seems to have persisted right up to the outbreak of the Pacific War. Take for example, Sasaki Kuni's juvenile novel *Kushin no gakuyū (The story of a troubled schoolfriend)*, in *The Shonen Kurabu*.[6] This tells the story of a youth who was the school friend of a child from a noble family, that of a count. This count's family were formerly *daimyō*, and the youth's ancestors were formerly feudal retainers. An old man called Anzai is their principal tutor and supervises the family teachers. This old fellow is a stickler for the correct way of doing things, but says nothing when the school results of the count's eldest son are poor. The eldest son, he is convinced, must be above petty and trivial consideration. When the eldest son's school marks are tioned, he is embarrassed and says, 'Young master, so long as you are confident that you can obtain full marks in all your examinations—that's enough'. What he meant was, 'If you obtain zero, then zero is all right; and if you fail, that's all right, too'. Whatever happened, the eldest son was going to be the count's heir and compared with the fact of being the eldest son, school marks and failures in examinations were trivial. But this same tutor was very pernickety about the marks of the second and third sons. The episode shows how deeply rooted in Japan was the idea 'eldest son, least clever'.

NOTES

1. Joei is the name of the era (1232–33), in which 'Jo' stands for stability and 'ei' for long, connoting a time of stability and well-being.
2. Toyotomi Hideyoshi (1537–98), one of the great figures in Japanese history, was born the son of a footsoldier named Kinoshita Yaemon, who was in the service of Oda Nobuhide, whose son, Oda Nobunaga, Hideyoshi presented himself to in 1558. He was quickly taken into Nobunaga's favour and achieved victory with him against Imagawa Yoshimoto, who was advancing on Kyoto in the battle of Okehazama (1560). From then on Hideyoshi became, successively, general under Nobunaga, and after his death Master of most of Japan's central prefectures. He later gained control of Northern and Southern territories and established the military reunification of Japan and the beginning of a new feudal hierarchy.
3. Oda Nobunaga (1534–82) initiated the 16th-century reunification of Japan, after one hundred years of internal strife, which was completed after his death by Hideyoshi. Nobunaga's origins were not from the higher levels of the military aristocracy; however, his father was a Sengoku Daimyo, Lord of Nagoya Castle. In 1574, Nobunaga accepted the status of an imperial noble, and in 1577 ascended to the third highest position in the hierarchy of the Imperial Court's official posts—that of Minister of the Right. However, he resigned all of these courtly titles and was finally offered the appointment of shogun, which was never settled due to his sudden and violent death at Honnoji Temple in Kyoto. Nobunaga had arrived there on his way to the Chugoku front campaign, and during a party held for some of the highest nobles of the Imperial Court, Akechi Mitsuhide, leader of the expedition, turned away from the road to Chugoku, and in an act of subterfuge, opened fire on Honnoji. After securing the safety of all women, Nobunaga,

badly wounded, retreated into the depths of the burning temple, where he finally disembowled himself.

4. Tokugawa Ieyasu (1542–1616) was born of Matsudaira Hirotada, a petty chieftain, allegedly descended from the Minamoto House, who was engaged in desperate efforts to fight off incursions from the neighbouring Oda family. To help in an alliance with his powerful neighbours to the East, the Imagawa of Suruga Province, Matsudaira offered his four-year-old son, Ieyasu as hostage. However, Ieyasu was captured on his way there by troops from the Oda Castle at Nagoya and remained there until a truce was called in 1549. However, the alliance with Imagawa still demanded a security, and Ieyasu remained with them for 12 years. When Oda Nobunaga attacked the Imagawa house in 1560, Ieyasu took the opportunity to return to his ancestral castle and assume command of his father's old vassals. After Nobunaga's death, Ieyasu reached a compromise with his successor Hideyoshi, with whom an uneasy alliance was maintained until Hideyoshi's death. In 1603 Ieyasu assumed the title of Seii Tai Shogun (meaning: barbarian-subduing generalissimo) which entitled him to speak for the Emperor on national affairs and held him personally responsible for the safety of the realm. Thus the Tokugawan Shogunate (1603–1867) began.

5. *The Abridged History of the Eighteen Dynasties.*
6. A boy's monthly.

12 The Meaning of the Meiji Restoration and the History of the Showa Period

WHY THE EDO (TOKUGAWA) SHOGUNATE COLLAPSED SO EASILY

The Tokugawa Shogunate, which thrust aside ability in this fashion, nonetheless produced a country which was exceptional in the modern world. A country with a population exceeding 20 million and no wars either within its own frontiers, or overseas, survived intact for two and a half centuries. There was nothing like it anywhere in the world. It is not surprising that the Edo period is of great interest to scholars of Japan. The foundations of the shogunate appeared to be as solid as a rock. Authority was strong and not one *daimyō* harboured thoughts of resistance.

However, all that was turned topsy-turvy in an instant. Why? The arrival of the black ships forced the shogunate to seriously question the basic premise of its existence. In the sixth year of Kaei (1853), the American Commodore Perry, with four black ships, appeared off Uraga. Those ships carried big guns. The Japanese had used big guns to make war 250 years before and knew their power. They had of their own accord put a stop to the manufacture of big guns and fire-arms. So they understood at once that the black ships from America could bombard Edo, that there was no defence strategy against them, that foreigners could land anywhere in Japan and occupy it, and so on.

At this point, the major premise of the shogunate collapsed. Ieyasu had put an end to the ability-principle and had converted Japan completely into an agrarian society which had functioned perfectly because the great agrarian premise was the 'feeling of security'. If the country were closed to outsiders, Japan had no need to make war anywhere, and there was no fear of her being attacked. So it was possible to govern the whole of Japan according to agrarian concepts. But when the black ships came, the danger of invasion arose and there was no way of stopping it. The system proved to be useless and the people ceased to obey it.

In the first year of Manen (1860), Ii Naosuke, the Chief Minister in the shogunate, was attacked and killed by wandering samurai outside the Sakurada-Gate of Edo Castle. Only seven years later the great decree of the Meiji Restoration, which restored Imperial rule, was promulgated. Hardly ten years were needed for the absolutely powerful shogunate to disappear.

THE ELDER STATESMEN OF THE MEIJI PERIOD PRODUCED FROM THE SOIL OF AN EQUESTRIAN SOCIETY

The Meiji government which took its place was, naturally enough, a society based on the equestrian principle, the 'ability principle'. It is well known that many of the elder statesmen of the Meiji Restoration were low-ranking samurai. Ito Hirobumi, who became the first Prime Minister, was a farmer from Choshu in Southern Honshu, whose family, in his father's generation, had, as was traditionally permissible, bought the status of *ashigaru* (foot soldier under authentic samurai) and was first raised to the lowest rank of samurai in Ito Hirobumi's generation. This man became Prime Minister four times during the Meiji period.

Similarly, Yamagata Aritomo, an army general and Field Marshal, who twice became Prime Minister, was the son of the assistant of a warehouse superintendent of lower rank than a foot-soldier of Choshu. Because these two men were raised to the peerage and were decorated with the order of the Chrysanthemum, first class, we should compare their success with that of Toyotomi Hideyoshi. We have, purely fortuitously, used examples of men born in Choshu, but the same thing applies to men born in Satsuma. If these men had been born in the Genroku era (1688–1704) or the

Bunka-Bunsei era (1804–30), they would have been plain
foot-soldiers and nothing else. When the elder statesmen of
the Restoration were criticised by the advocates of freedom
and people's rights (jiyu minken), they are said to have
retorted, 'we took power on horseback', which must have
been their real feeling. Certainly, 300 years after the close
of the Civil War period, the Meiji Restoration was once
again a period of equestrian ideology.

To explore their ways of thinking, let us select one or two
examples of Chinese-style poems by Ito Hirobumi, whose
portrait until recently figured on our thousand-yen notes.
Let me observe that from an early age Hirobumi had been
fond of poetry in the Chinese manner and had some skill in
it. He used 'Shumpo' (Spring Furrow) as his pen-name and
he refers to himself as 'Master of the Tower of the Ocean
Waves' in an allusion to his residence in Oiso, which was
called Sorokaku, 'Tower of the Ocean Waves'.

> The stout heart in its splendour reaches across the
> heavens;
> Who else, in this eastern country, can foster the might of
> empire?
> In the tall tower, three cups of *sake* are drained;
> The heroes of our land shrink in my eyes.

This poem is from Hirobumi's early years but throughout
his life he never doubted that he would be a great hero. His
confidence that he, and no other, in the Japan of those
days, would raise up the authority of the Emperor is clear
from these lines. No such poem could have been written by
a man of the Tokugawa Period.

However, the equestrian atmosphere of the Meiji period
rapidly disappeared from the bureaucracy and the armed
forces after the Russo-Japanese War. There was no army
on the continent of Asia capable of confronting the Japanese
Army. That Army had not suffered a single defeat at the
hands of the Russians; and had not the Russians been
victorious over Napoleon? As for the Navy, while the
Japanese Fleet sent almost the whole of the Baltic Fleet to
the bottom, it lost not a single man-of-war. No fleet capable
of confronting the Imperial Combined fleet existed east of
Suez or west of Panama.

This merely helped to bring into being the conviction that the land of the gods was indestructible.

So the 'feeling of security' ran right through the armed forces. This feeling of security allowed the old agrarian way of thought to emerge once more. At all events, the tradition which had survived from prehistoric times, and the 'Don Peasant' nature which had been refined for 300 years of Tokugawa rule, emerged once more in a system which appeared to be indestructible, once the Meiji era came to an end. The Meiji equestrian ideology proved to be the exception.

In disputes over seniority which revolved around two issues: 'What year did you enter this office?', 'What's your degree?', the greatest attention was paid to preserving harmony inside the respective office. And I have tried to show how that produced a pattern of movement in which, in order to preserve that harmony, Japan rushed headlong into a great war which she had no chance of winning.

WHY DID SO MANY DISTURBANCES BREAK OUT IN THE EARLY SHOWA PERIOD (1925–40) WITH ITS AGRARIAN IDEOLOGY?

Perhaps one doubt emerges at this point. The question might well be asked, 'Although no samurai uprisings occurred in the Tokugawa period, why did so many military uprisings occur in the Showa period which were of a similar agrarian type—the 15 May 1931 Incident, the 26 February 1936 Incident, the Manchurian Incident, the China Incident?' Uprisings occur in an agrarian society when a feeling of crisis supervenes and the 'feeling of security' is damaged. So what contributed to the background of the military uprisings? The major issues were the anti-Japanese immigration laws of the United States (in 1910s and 1920s), and the London Treaty of 1930.

The movement of hostility towards the Japanese immigrants in the United States arose just after the Russo-Japanese War and culminated in the anti-Japanese immigration laws of 1924. These laws were the result of a policy of blatant racial discrimination and deliberately introduced exceptions to the Constitution in which the right of citizenship is vested in people who have been born in the United States. In the amendment made to the Constitution, children of United States citizens descended from Japanese immigrants were refused the right to be Americans, even if they had been born in the United States. This was a slap in the face for the Japanese, who had won the Russo-Japanese War, who had participated in the Peace Treaty of World War I, and who boasted of being on the same footing as other nations.[1] Because of this, our country's traditional pro-American foreign policy ran into severe difficulties.

Had this been all, things might still have been all right. But in 1930 the London Treaty was signed: the ratio of naval strengths became 5.5.3. respectively for Great Britain, the United States and Japan. The Washington Conference of 1921 had reduced armaments and limited the building of battleships and aircraft carriers, but there remained the possibility of developing a speciality because submarines and other auxiliary ships were outside the purview of the restrictions, so it seemed likely that somehow our defence strength could be maintained.

The London Conference, however, enforced severe restrictions across all classes of ships up to and including auxiliary vessels, and to accept this meant that in the future Japan would inevitably be defeated by Great Britain and the United States.

The notion of securing the supremacy of the white man in perpetuity seemed evident, on the one hand, in publicising and legalising racial discrimination against Japan, and on the other, creating conditions for the Japanese Navy which would inevitably lead to its defeat. Disturbances broke out in Japan. Furthermore, in China, backed by Great Britain and the United States, there was a boycott of Japanese goods and there was also retaliation against Japanese citizens. This was the situation when young Navy and Army officers and right-wing elements, overwhelmed by a feeling of crisis, took matters into their own hands and disregarded the higher-ranking officers of their own services.

Abe Genki's *Showa Doran no Shinso* (*The Truth about the Showa Disturbances*)[2] shows in detail how the London treaty triggered off what became known as the 'Showa disturbances'. Abe was Minister for Home Affairs (Interior) at the end of the war and at the time of the disturbances occupied a strategic position in the Special Police Division for maintenance of public order. Nevertheless, the Treaty did not have the same impact on the Showa period as the black ships did on the Tokugawa Shogunate and there was no clean sweep of the whole structure of society. Gradually Japan was led to embark on her great war, with her agrarian ideology intact. Violent extremist elements were restrained and harmony preserved without the older generation foregoing their agrarian principles and actually repressing the uprisings of the younger. The way they dealt with this situation, with the issues of war or peace, finally drew them into a great war.

The essential feature of the equestrian ideology is that there is a feeling of insecurity deep within us: 'We don't know when the collapse will come.'

The patriots of the Meiji Restoration of 1868 never rid themselves of the fear of not knowing when they might be conquered and colonised by a foreign country. This was perfectly natural, for both the Choshu and the Satsuma clans had had experience of being thoroughly whipped by the armed forces of foreign countries at the end of the shogunate. But the leaders of Showa Japan were fundamentally at ease, and continued to think, 'the land of the gods is indestructible, so somehow it will be all right in the end'. Looked at coldly, it is clear that even when defeat was only a question of time, Japanese military professionals were still waiting for the coming of the 'wind from heaven'.[3] This, as I have pointed out, is the feeling of security that lies at the root of the agrarian ideology.

THE END OF THE SHORT-LIVED POST-WAR EQUESTRIAN SOCIETY AND THE ENSUING YEARS

For a short time in the post-1945 period, the equestrian concept came back into its own. The nobility had been done away with, and the big commercial combines had been dissolved. Japan's way ahead was uncertain. The Prime Minister (at this juncture) had been selected on the ability principle, as we have said earlier, or at any rate on the 'ability-to-speak-English principle'. And among the personnel of the civil service, in particular the public servants in the regions and in the field of primary and secondary education there were not many gifted candidates. There was a fairly conspicuous tendency for everyone to choose highly-paid professions, even risky ones, in preference to a stable bureaucratic career with a low salary.

But post-war equestrian tendencies were, I feel, finished symbolically by the Lockheed affair. Both the former Prime Minister, Mr Kakuei Tanaka, and the super-rich entrepreneur, Mr Osano Kenji, were mere private soldiers when Japan was defeated. They were at the bottom of the pile in the Japanese Army. Both had experience of the wounds and diseases of war; neither had any academic record. However, one became a Prime Minister of the conservative party and the other an industrialist with a huge private fortune.

The short post-war period was a period of equestrian ideology. Remember that when Mr Tanaka became Prime Minister, everybody said, 'A latter-day Hideyoshi!' The establishment of the Suzuki Cabinet seems to have been of an opposite kind.

It seemed then as if Japan was returning to an agrarian type of society. University graduates began to want to become civil servants or teachers again. Another oil crisis had been weathered, and a sense of security returned. Where this feeling of security exists, the ideology becomes agrarian: that is the lesson of history.

Of course, the energy crisis has not just gone away: there is still an urgent need to increase reserves for an emergency through employing nuclear power, until the next energy source appears. Even though this has been recognised by many, the feeling of security prevails and there is even opposition to installing nuclear generators.

A people which can live in an agrarian way with a deep inner sense of security is, in many ways, a happy people. But if harmony is valued above everything else as in the last great war, there is a danger that the whole nation could be dragged along into some awful catastrophe.

The phrase, 'earthquakes come when everyone's forgotten about them' sums it up: we seem to be able to forget the cataclysms and catastrophes produced by war. Perhaps this means that such catastrophes take place so seldom that we can afford to forget them.

NOTES

1. On this question, see my article 'The history of the love-hate relationship between Japan and the United States', in *Seigi no jidai* (*The Era of Justice*) (Bungei Shunju, 1977).
2. Abe Genki, *Showa Doran no Shinso* (*The Truth About the Showa Disturbances*) (Hara Shobe, 1978).
3. 'Wind from heaven' (literally 'divine wind') or 'Kamikaze' is a term applied to a strong prevailing wind off the coast of Ise. In modern usage it refers to the storms that destroyed invading Mongol armadas on two occasions in 1274 and 1281 which represented to the Japanese of that time the divine intervention of the gods from Ise Shrine. 'Kamikaze' was also the name applied to the suicide pilots of World War II.

Part IV
The Age of the Japanese Idea

13 The Spirit of Commerce and its Effect on the Japanese

GREAT BRITAIN, THE PRIME EXAMPLE OF A TRADING COUNTRY OF MODERN TIMES

There have been basically two kinds of exceptions in the history of Japan as an agrarian society. One being a specific *period*—the Civil War period, the Meiji Restoration, the post-war era; and the other being more concerned with social organisation and in particular the genesis of 'trade'. This can be studied in the history of other agrarian peoples.

Let us consider the prime example of Great Britain as *the* trading country of modern times. The Germanic peoples who migrated to this region were the Angles and Saxons. There are still such people today living on the continent of Europe, known as 'Angeln' in Jutland, in Germany as 'Sachsen'; and these were originally agrarian peoples. The primitive Sachsen people who were their ancestors belonged to the 'Ingveonen' tribe, and their tribal god was the 'god of Ing', the earth god. This group migrated to England halfway through the fifth century.

We should call them agrarian only to start with, for commerce grew with the increase in population and with the raising of cultural levels. According to the Venerable Bede, who wrote the first great history of England, various peoples had come to trade by sea and land to the place called 'London' by the first half of the eighth century. About halfway through the 11th century Duke William of Normandy successfully invaded England and became King and the charter he subsequently gave to the city of London, legal historians say, 'is to an extraordinary degree both prudent and parsimonious.' The citizens' rights of inheritance were guaranteed, but no special right of self-government was acknowledged.

In his son Henry I's time (1100–35), London was recognised as independent, raised to the same status as a county and permitted to choose its own chief governor and chief justice. Its citizens could not be summoned to a tribunal outside the city walls and were granted various special rights. By the end of the 12th century the mayoral office had emerged and in the reign of Edward IV (1442–83) a charter was granted acknowledging London as a corporation in its own right.

In this way, in many foreign countries, what are called 'cities', with their special charters, gradually increased in number and became completely autonomous bodies. Even today, for instance, cities on the continent of Europe, like Hamburg and Bremen with populations of 1 800 000 and 600 000 respectively, have the same status as a *Land* state in the German Federal Republic with a tradition dating from the days of the cities of Hanseatic League

A citizen is distinguished by the fact that he is not subject to any feudal lord. Even today, the Queen cannot enter the central part of London called 'The City' without authorisation of the Lord Mayor, although this is, of course, only a formality. This shows the degree of respect for the citizens' rights.

THE ORIGINS OF COMMERCE—JAPAN'S CITIES. THE CASE OF SAKAI

What happened in Japan?

There are records of a trader called Kichiji, coming from the province of Mutsu in the days of Minamoto Yoshitsune (d. 1189), though we can hardly describe this as the genesis of a merchant class. The Kamakura Shogunate forbade the sale of *sake* but in the fourth year of the reign of Hojo Tokiyori (1251) permission was granted for one jar only per household to be distilled. This seems to have been the beginning of trade. Tokiyori had, it is true, authorised a trading area in Kamakura the previous year, but there is no comparison between the scale of the trading area of Kamakura and that of London or the Hanseatic cities.

However 'trade' rapidly extended in the latter half of the Kamakura period, and at first gave rise to friction with the agrarian-style government. The 'ordinance of benevolent rule' in the fifth year of Einin (1297), in which debts were annulled without any compensation, should probably be considered as an indication of this. At the start there was official trade with the Sung dynasty of China, and afterwards private trade with the Yuan, and organisations of commerce and industry resembling guilds emerged. We should think of the time from halfway through the Kamakura period right through the Ashikaga Shogunate (14th and 15th centuries) as a time in which Japan's population increased and her cultural standards rose to the level at which commerce developed rapidly.

The disturbances which started in the first year of Ōnin (1467) mark the beginning of the Civil War period, but even though the government was in a turmoil there was a remarkable development of commerce. As the whole country was run on equestrian lines in the civil wars, commerce had a certain affinity with the trend of the times. It was vital to be able to exercise command, to judge one's own talents for management without any basis for deep feelings of inner security. The case of Sakai, located near present-day Osaka, is typical. It grew rapidly as a commercial city from the end of the Kamakura period and numbered 10 000 households in the Ashikaga period. Then during the civil wars it grew even faster and the senior merchants, like those who became aldermen in the City of London, operated a structure not unlike the English corporation.

These senior merchants (the etymology of 'alderman' is, in fact, 'elder man') were big businessmen who called themselves *egōshū* (companions of the assembly) or *nayashū* (companions of the warehouses). Sakai's most prosperous period was in the 1560s when Nobunaga gradually began to make his mark. No *daimyō* yet ruled the country as a whole and it was possible to trade freely. The Christian missionaries first began to arrive in Japan during this period and Sakai reminded them of Venice. They took it to be a small republic governed by its own ministers.

The height of Sakai's prosperity corresponds in the West to the early years of Elizabeth I (1533–1603) when England, which might have been considered up to that time little more than an island fragment of Europe, made a quantum leap into becoming the greatest trading nation in the world. So, about four centuries ago, around 1560, London and Sakai stood together on the same start-line. After that, London's development made great strides, but Sakai's growth came to a halt, rather like a garden plant which has been lopped. Why was this?

The reason was that Japan's equestrian society came to an end. In the 12th year of Eiroku (1569), Nobunaga brought Sakai under his direct control. Next, Hideyoshi made Osaka his principal seat and compelled many of the Sakai townspeople to move to it. Sakai's hitherto autonomous regime perished; but economic prosperity continued because both Nobunaga and Hideyoshi were equestrian types and were not hostile towards trade.

When, however, a government appeared with the agrarian concepts of the Tokugawa Shogunate, and went to the lengths of making Japan a strictly closed country, overseas trade was carried on under rigid control; Sakai therefore could not continue to develop as London did. Of course, cultural standards continued to rise even under the Tokugawa Shogunate, and commercial activity flourished in Osaka and Edo because there was a fair-sized population. But the shogunate itself was biased against trade.

THE THREE GREAT TOKUGAWA REFORMS: A POLICY OF ANTI-COMMERCIAL PRESSURE BASED ON ENVY

Since the peasant was aware that 'farming is the bedrock of the nation', his instinct was to look down upon the merchant. At the same time, he inevitably envied the merchant, who was not restricted by the land, managed his own affairs by his own talents, wore fine clothes, ate delicious food and lived in a clean and well-kept house. That complex of feelings has begun to diminish today, now that daily life in the country is no different from life in the towns, there are any number of cars, and agricultural machinery is fully developed; but up to about 1955 it was still evident.

In war-time, the people were mobilised for labour service and compulsory help was organised for farmers. The townfolk began to experience shortages and the arrogance of farmers made life very tough. How often did we hear, in the mouths of countryfolk, such phrases as 'These city folk never go out to work in the muddy paddy-fields. If they think they'll get anything to eat from us, they've got another think coming!'

That did not stop them wanting to wear the clothes the townspeople wore, or to have the things townspeople had. Contemporary psychology might term this phenomenon 'ambivalence'. Townspeople were felt to be 'shady characters' ('usan kusage'). The samurai of the Tokugawa period who shared the feeling of the peasants always looked down on townspeople as 'shady characters'. On the slightest pretext they would exert pressure on them and impose restrictions on luxuries, on a high standard of living. And they were overjoyed when they succeeded in crushing cultural activities. The results can be seen in the Kyōhō reform of the Eighth Shogun Yoshimune (d. 1745),[1] the Kansei reform of Matsudaira Sadanobu (retired from the office 1793),[2] and the Tenpō reform of Mizuno Tadakuni (d. 1851).[3] Even in today's high-school textbooks, these periods are still referred to as 'the good government of Kyōhō, 'the good government of Kansei', and are praised and held up for admiration as good times in Japanese history.

The reality is rather different. It is that of a shogunate with basically a peasant psychology, depressing the rising standard of living of the townspeople and satisfying its grudges against them by complacently proclaiming, 'We have done away with corruption and luxury'. It invoked a principle of righteousness—the prohibition of luxury—so that those in power, whose authority was not based on the exercise of ability, could crush those they envied, who produced wealth by the exercise of their own talents. 'We cannot allow the townspeople to live extravagantly', they thought, 'when the peasants are poor'. The prime mover behind all this was the shogunate itself, which collected the annual land tax from the peasants. When Yoshimune succeeded to the shogunate in 1716, the treasury of Edo Castle, which must have been crammed with gold in the days of Ieyasu, was almost empty. Yoshimune decided to replenish it, and promptly boosted taxes by one fifth. The rice produced had been divided 4/10 for the lord and 6/10 for the people since the shogunate was founded. But he changed the rate to 5/10 for the lords and 5/10 for the people, thus depriving the peasantry. More than that, he ordered an increased levy of one hundred *koku* (1 koku = 5.1 US bushels) of rice per 10 000 *koku* on all the nobility (which, of course, again rebounded on the peasants). He also issued an amazing edict making the repayment of loans unnecessary when rice was cheap. The debtors (samurai) could repay their loans when the price of rice went up again. The purpose of this was to allow the samurai, who had the rice, to make a profit at the expense of their victims, the townspeople.

Of course, such a short-sighted move led the economy into chaos, because the time came when no one was ready to lend money, and in their turn the samurai found themselves in a mess. The currency deteriorated, too, at the end of Yoshimune's rule, and the gold content of the *koban*—the gold coin of the Edo period—was tremendously reduced, being in the 1730s only 3/5ths what it had been in the 1580s; that is, from a hundred old *koban* dollars, 179 new dollars were made. As the people were compelled to honour the old *koban* and the new at the same value, it was a case of absolute highway robbery.

THE EDO PERIOD: THE HATRED OF ABILITY AND ADMIRATION FOR CULTURAL REFINEMENT

I do not wish to go too deeply into the government of Yoshimune but I should point out that this man was highly esteemed and has been praised by historians since the Tokugawa period, even up to the present time. This is because he proved to be acceptable to an agrarian-type people in two respects. Firstly, Yoshimune was sober and earnest. He behaved with discretion and had few faults in his private life. This does not mean that he had no concubines, but he kept to the common-sense limits of that time, did not indulge in extravagant living and aimed to be impartial. He was certainly a cultivated man and ruled as wisely as he knew how. When the wandering samurai, Yamanouchi Kōnai, criticised Yoshimune and presented him with a remonstrance proclaiming 'You cannot very well govern the whole country as if you were governing a county in Kishū, Yoshimune was indignant but did not show his feelings and tried his best only to praise what had been said. He was interested in farming, and decided to try transplanting waxtree seeds from Kyūshū and cultivating sugar in Kantō. He was not so much incompetent as more the victim of a number of maladroit policies; but the historians of the shogunate do not make an issue of his ability. He was a cultivated gentleman of the agrarian type.

The second thing which enhanced the popularity of Yoshimune was his direct rule as shogun. For two previous generations of shogun, the sixth, Ienobu (d. 1712) and the seventh, Ietsuga (who died at the age of eight in 1716) the government had been in the hands of Manabe Akifusa and Arai Hakuseki.[4]

If the object of government is to raise the standard of living, then Manabe and Hakuseki were very skilful administrators. However, the samurai of those days disapproved of their influence.

Both Manabe and Hakuseki, without regard to lineage, reached the very heart of shogunal power by their ability alone. The samurai, for whom class was determined by lineage, were hardly overjoyed by this. When Yoshimune became shogun by inheritance and men whose ability had brought success withdrew from public life, the samurai were overjoyed, and the history written during this period of the shogunate turned into a monochromatic Yoshimune-worship. Histories about the shogunate which the shogunate had written were held up as what is called 'good quality contemporary material', and even now historians speak of the 'good government of Kyōhō'. Yoshimune's popularity is an excellent indication of the disfavour in which men of ability were held and of the admiration lavished on the cultivated gentleman of the mid-Tokugawa period.

We have primary source material from this time which reveals the discrepancy between recorded history and privately held views. The consort of the Sixth Shogun Ienobu was of the House of Konoe, and her father, Konoe Motohiro, was much concerned about the situation in Edo. He would have talks with anyone who had travelled from Kyoto to Edo, write down what they told him, and make extracts of letters from Edo.

Let me cite two examples of these, written around the time of Yoshimune's Kyōhō reform (around 1720). 'Poverty in the city of Edo. Not a single newly-built house of a *daimyō* or lesser feudal lord in the city; all is thatch and thorn.' 'There is mistrust for the ways of government, the age is full of the people's hatred.'

To say that not a single new house had been put up in Edo shows the extent of the depression. When houses were not built, vacant lots increased in the city and grass grew everywhere. Yet, in spite of this, Yoshimune was very popular among us, and we know why. The source of his popularity was in the *fudai-daimyō* (hereditary lordly vassals of the Tokugawa) and the *hatamoto* (literally 'flag-bearers', hereditary direct non-lordly vassals).

THE TOWNSMEN WHO BEGAN TO DEFY THE SAMURAI

Unlike the peasants and the samurai, the townsmen relied on their own judgement, which depended on mutual credit between business associates, so they could not afford to be negligent. Ability and credit continuously increased as a result of their own efforts. In the latter half of the Tokugawa period, however often the agrarian-style shogunate oppressed the equestrian-style merchants by the force of authority, we can see the oppression receding step by step. We know that townsmen respected the value of credit in those days, but let me tell one story which emphasises this respect from a purely human point of view. A certain thrifty man in Osaka saved the sum of three or four hundred *ryō*. He valued it as much as life itself. To prepare against the ten thousand to one chance of the worst happening, and thinking the House of Mitsui offered most security, he obtained an introduction from an aquaintance and deposited his money with Mitsui. Every time this man went to Mitsui, they showed him the money he had deposited kept as it was, rolled up unused, and he was paid interest on it.

So, if Mitsui were entrusted with the savings of a commoner, they safeguarded them unused, yet still generously paying the interest twice a year. On the other hand, the Shogun of that time resorted to borrowing the rice-stipend (the *kirimai*, or rice given as stipend to the samurai) of the direct vassals (*hatamoto*), created an official value for it less than the worth of current prices for rice and strove hard to profit by a rake-off. It was the house of Mitsui, the townsmen, which gave benefits to people who saved. The signs are that Japan in this period was moving in the direction of the cultivation of ability.[5]

Matsudaira Tadanobu's Kansei reform (1789) bears a startling resemblance to Yoshimune's Kyōhō reform. Though it is termed 'the good government of Kansei', it is a sterile and pernicious reform.

Before Tadanobu came on the scene, the two mediocre and stupid shoguns, the ninth, Ieshige, and the tenth, Ieharu, had employed as their counsellor Tanuma Okitsugu. He was a man of ability who rose from a very low rank and became a personal steward of the shogun and a powerful member of the shogun's Council of Elders. He became, as a result, the object of severe criticism by those who believed status should be acquired by inheritance, and was thrust aside.[6] After Tanuma's overthrow, Matsudaira Tadanobu was welcomed by men of the same stamp as had welcomed Yoshimune. His economic ordinances were nothing other than the exerting of pressure on commerce. High-class confectionery, costly clothing, elaborate firemen's uniforms, luxurious Nō costumes, were banned. Sets of ritual bows and arrows, costly dolls for the Boy's Festival, dolls taller than nine inches high, battledores, doll accoutrements, ornamental bodkins and hairpins, combs, pipes and other objects involving the use of gold, or elaborate craftsmanship, were banned. Certain kinds of books and novels, newly published woodblock prints, were also prohibited. The inevitable result of such draconian prohibition was unemployment on a large scale.

The idle or the unemployed were assembled and put to work reclaiming over 50 000 square metres of land around the present Ishikawajima along the shores of Tokyo Bay. We would call this, today, a forced labour concentration camp. Tadanobu applied to Japan as a whole a measure which was more appropriate to solving the problems of a local area. It was parallel with Yoshimune's doing in Edo what might have been appropriate in the county of Kishu.

Yoshimune's policy had endured for close on 30 years, but Tadanobu's, carried out against townspeople who had known the flavour of Edo culture at its great heights in the Tanuma days, began at once to crack visibly at the seams. He held on to political power for only six years. Peasant riots had broken out during the 'good government of Kyōhō' (1716–36), and ironically during the 'good government of Kansei' (1789–1801) violence erupted in the city of Edo for the first time. The reader can judge how appropriate was the use of the term 'good government' to describe these periods.

Yet despite all of this Matsudaira Tadanobu is a very popular figure among the historians of the Tokugawa house. The reason is, exactly as in the case of Yoshimune, that he was a cultivated man, an extraordinarily likeable individual, learned and refined. Indeed, he was something of a man of letters. It presented no problem for the ruling establishment with their agrarian mode of thoughts that he was, politically, totally impotent.

ENVY IN AN AGRARIAN SOCIETY: THE MOTIVE FORCE WHICH DESTROYS CIVILISATION

Nothing daunted, the shogunate put through the Tenpo Reform in 1841 (the 12th year of Tenpo), again attempting to destroy commerce root and branch. The shogun's chief administrator Mizuno Tadakuni (d. 1851) introduced this reform, the aim of which was to return to the measures of the Kyōhō and Kansei 'good government'. Failure was inevitable from the start.

Because Tadakuni felt he had to transform Edo eventually into the wilderness of the days of Ieyasu, he seems to have been determined to destroy luxury and crush the towns-people. 'Rescripts are showering down like rain' was the criticism of his contemporaries. Prohibitions followed one another in rapid succession and were enforced. There seem-ed no end to the interdictions, everything was forbidden which, in the slightest way, smacked of culture or of a high standard of living: splendid houses, highly expensive cakes, stone lanterns costing more than ten *ryō*, gold-decorated ritual bows and arrows, battledores, dolls higher than nine inches high (yet again), women's hairdressers, women teachers of social accomplishments, barbers' shops, coloured curtains used as shop signs, highly ornate sign-boards, *habutae*-silk, silk crepe, satin, imported goods.

If you wore a luxurious kimono, government officials ripped it from you, even in the street. It was, quite literally, highway robbery. The study of European civilisation through the medium of the Dutch language was forbidden, the penalty for defiance being execution; Torii Yōzō, the second son of Hayashi Daigaku-no-kami (Chief of Confu-cian Studies for the shogun), the man entrusted with the supervision of these measures, was consumed by a burning envy towards scholars of Western learning.

Another measure by Mizuno Tadakuni abrogated the special rights of the *tokumi-donya*, the associations of guilds formed for the transport of goods between Osaka and Edo: anyone was allowed to trade freely between two cities. Although at first sight this seems a liberal measure, it originated in an out-and-out hatred of trade and carriers of merchandise, and its upshot was purely destructive. No alternative schemes were put forward. A trading system which had developed naturally and spontaneously for more than two centuries since the start of the Tokugawa Shogunate was destroyed in one fell swoop: merchandise could not be moved, currency ceased to circulate, the con-ventions of agreements were nullified, prices rose as goods became scarce, and the people suffered. So the Tenpo Reform came to an end in less than two years and Mizuno was overthrown. When the news of his downfall became known, thousands of townspeople laid siege to his house and began hurling stones at it. Soldiers had to be called out to prevent it from being destroyed.

Yet there is one other thing about the Tenpo Reforms which must not be forgotten. The top men of the shogunate and the *daimyōs* may have abandoned Mizuno quite soon, but even after his downfall the lower officials backed his policy. So Abe Masahiro, who became a member of the shogun's Council of Elders in Mizuno's place, found it difficult to obtain support. This shows how much the lower shogunate officials, who had a hard life, hated and envied the townspeople. If we look at the Tenpo Reform, we will be amazed to see points of resemblance, to a surprising degree, with the petty restrictive ordinances of World War II. Those who executed the ordinances restricting consumer goods in war-time were, I imagine, peasant-born, or at any rate their parents or grand-parents were peasants. The agrarian envy and hatred of merchants and businessmen goes very deep in Japan. Even in a mass-consumer society such as we have at present in Japan, on odd occasions the theory of 'Trade as Original Sin' rears its ugly head. When there are shortages of daily necessities, people may do a bit of panic-buying, but on the quiet, they will still lay the blame on the shops and the means of distribution rather than admit responsibility. Some time ago, when disturbances arose as the result of such shortages, the City of Tokyo under Governor Minobe publicly criticised a certain detergent company, without any foundation, merely because a complaint had been made against that company, for Governor Minobe was a man of agrarian notions.

Anti-commercial feeling continued when the Tenpo Reform came to an end; one thing the shogunate had no settled policy about was wholesale dealers, despite the fact that the people of Edo were groaning under a shortage of commodities, and that it was a matter of urgency for restoration of wholesale dealers to be ordered. There were many who opposed it, fearing that the merchants would become rich again. Not only were the Edo townsfolk troubled by shortages of goods, they were also short of cash and, to make matters worse, many of the businessmen and merchants who would have responded to the shogunate's order for government funds had disappeared for good. However, in the first year of Kaei (1848), without repealing the law for the abolition of wholesale dealers, what was called a 'provisional order' was promulgated which, inevitably, permitted the restoration of wholesale dealers by means of a temporary regulation only. Even after that, discussion continued in the shogunate. Finally, however, in the fourth year of Kaei (1851), the tenth year after the Tenpo Reform, the wholesale dealers' syndicates were authorised to be restored as they had been before the Bunka-Bunsei period (that is, the first years of the 19th century). When the wholesale dealers were restored, brokerage and retail sales were organised as before and this state of affairs lasted until the Meiji Restoration of 1868.

THE PATTERN OF DESTRUCTION OF JAPAN'S COMMERCIAL WORLD IN 40-YEAR CYCLES

A glance at this simplified outline of the history of Japanese commerce will show that Japan's trade has been destroyed cyclically, as a rule once every 40 years. The destructive power was always the shogunate and its agrarian notions. From Sakai's prosperity in the 16th century, if there had been no prohibitions, no 'closed country' policy, and no Kyōhō, Kansei or Tenpo reforms, by the end of the shogunate, Sakai and Osaka would have become commercial centres on a world-scale no whit inferior to London. Even under 'closed country' conditions, without the pressure on trade masquerading under the fair name of 'reform', the culture of the Edo townspeople would have spread its roots deeper. It would have produced a civilisation on a grander scale. But it was destroyed root and branch three times, once every 40 years, and there was no question of its extending, It is interesting, even so, that the periods of pressure on commerce were gradually reduced. The Kyōhō reform lasted 28 years, Kansei six, and Tenpo two. This shows how the shogunate, however much it hated merchants, had become more and more incapable of applying pressure on them.

The same thing can be seen, according to Ota Sik, in the pressures applied by government in the Soviet Union and in Eastern Europe. A professor at the Staff College of the

Central Committee of the Czechoslovakian Communist Party, head of the Economic Research Unit of the Academy of Sciences, Deputy Premier and Minister of Economics, Mr Sik had an extensive knowledge of the Communist sphere, both as an academic and as a practical administrator, and had several times investigated how goods tend to flow along commercial lines on the black market, how control decreases at each successive introduction. This recalls, does it not, the anti-trade policy of the Tokugawa period?

Communist countries, it may be said in passing, are an area ruled by an anti-commercial system. So commerce does not develop in these countries and it is almost impossible for them to produce commercial goods which can compete in the international market. It may be more accurate to say that the Communist revolution has succeeded where trade is undeveloped and the number of citizens with purchasing power is small. Moreover, in the case of the Soviet Union or China, we are speaking of vast territories, countries with a feeling of security in which self-sufficiency is by and large possible even though the people are poor, so long as they stay put. I have not studied the facts about them in detail, but it can be inferred that such countries have a strong agrarian ideology. Have they, I wonder, turned into societies with a strong spirit of envy and mutual surveillance? Whatever the recent political changes, there are few possibilities for talented young people to escape the system in these Communist countries. Human affairs will go on according to the palace policies and we may imagine that those who find it easy to maintain the harmony of the Party will win in the end.

The merchants of the Edo period had a feeling of crisis. They never knew when they might become bankrupt, however large their businesses. This must have seemed almost natural, given the nature of commerce. As a result of this feeling of insecurity, it not infrequently happened that heiresses were given in marriage to clerks of proven ability who became adopted sons of the family and were able to manage affairs efficiently. The property in such cases was divided so that the sons of the family, who might be less capable, had enough to live on according to their tastes, but in a sort of retirement, while they were still young. Even when the succession was reserved to the sons, inheritance by the eldest son was not strictly maintained, as it was in the samurai families and peasant families. The succession went to the most able, though care was taken to ensure that a comfortable life was possible for those with no responsibility in the business. With the ever-present danger of bankruptcy, an inflexible pattern of inheritance was not appropriate.

THE PRO-COMMERCE AND PRO-INDUSTRY POLICY OF THE MEIJI RESTORATION: THE REVIVAL OF THE ANTI-COMMERCIAL SPIRIT

The Meiji Restoration was, as I have said, a period of equestrian ideology. At the same time as the country was opened, Samuel Smiles' *Self-Help* (translated as *Saikoku-Risshi-Hen, The Book of Western Success*) was published in Japanese by Nakamura Keiu and sold more than a million copies at a time when Japan's population was 30 000 000. *Self-Help* was a book which seemed to crystallise the spirit of the age in which Great Britain led the world in trade. It had a tremendous influence in Japan at a time when the entire Japanese people were adopting more equestrian methods.

Although we must admit that the Japanese are fundamentally agrarian, it has been amply proved that when the situation becomes equestrian, great numbers of talented men appear in tune with the times. Such were the leaders of the Meiji period. Almost immediately, commercial Japan began to compete on the world stage; enterprises speedily emerged capable of challenging the developed countries. The fact that the marine transport companies (for example NYK Lines) and the general trading companies (the so-called sōgō shōsha) rapidly became the strongest companies in the world, demonstrates the ability of the Japanese people. Leaders like Shibusawa Eiichi sharpened the awareness of Japanese businessmen and industrialists to the level of the businessmen of Europe and the United States. He tried to extricate them from the concepts of the Edo tradition, from a society in which the hierarchy was: warrior, peasant, artisan, merchant. Even so, until the end of the Pacific War, it seemed that the warrior (the services and the bureaucracy) still ruled over the merchant and the artisan.

In that period from the Meiji Restoration onwards, when talent and ability were in free competition, a pattern emerged which might be termed 'the survival of the fittest'. When the law of the survival of the fittest operates too effectively, the difference between those with talent and those without seems excessive. This was why commerce and industry were attacked both by the left-wing and the right.

The Manchurian Incident (1931) occurred about 40 years after the promulgation of the Meiji Constitution (once again that 40 years cycle!) and the authorisation of free commercial and industrial activity. In Manchuria (Manchukuo) it was planned that enterprises connected with the *zaibatsu* (the large commercial and industrial conglomerates) should not be involved. The original notion of the soldiers who created Manchukuo was, apparently, to introduce into that country peasants from Japan and Korea. We know that these soldiers maintained close ties with their peasant roots and loathed commerce and industry. The Manchurian Railway was the most important concern in Manchuria, but being under the control of the military it was not an ordinary commercial enterprise.

Both political parties, Seiyūkai and Minseitō, had a base in the world of commerce and industry. The leaders of the Meiji Restoration had nothing against agriculture, but they were from the start men with equestrian concepts and understood perfectly well that the future prosperity of Japan lay in the promotion of commerce and industry and that, if these failed, the failure would extend to the armed services, too. In both the Sino-Japanese War (1894–98) and the Russo-Japanese War (1904–05) they were determined to buy battleships from the great trading powers such as Great Britain, and others.

In other words, they understood quite clearly that commercial and industrial power could be transformed into military power. So, when political parties were created, they based themselves unhesitatingly on commerce and industry.

THE ANTI-COMMERCIAL SPIRIT CONCEALED
BEHIND THE OPPRESSIVE TAXATION SYSTEM
OF THE PRESENT DAY

However, the feeling of security after the Russo-Japanese
War brought about once more a revival of the ways of
thinking proper to an agrarian society. We can understand
why the left-wing should attack the *zaibatsu* (the large
commercial and industrial conglomerates); but the new
right-wing did likewise. The left-wing was curbed by the
right-wing, which itself killed prominent businessmen like
Inoue Junnosuke (d. 1932) and Dan Takuma (d. 1932), as
well as the Prime Ministers Hamaguchi Osachi (d. 1931)
and Inukai Tsuyoshi (d. 1932), and others who were leaders
of political parties with a base in commerce and industry.
The right-wing and the young military officers of those
days claimed to represent the feelings of the peasantry;
their enemy was commerce and industry, particularly the
zaibatsu. The political parties were finally extinguished in
1940.

But the feeling of crisis over national survival in the
right-wing and among the young officers was not genuine.
They said they grieved for their country, but they were
confident in their hearts that there was no real danger of
Japan being destroyed; what they felt was sympathy with
the poor peasants and resentment over the inequitable
distribution of wealth.

The feeling of crisis among the Meiji Restoration leaders,
on the other hand, was a real one and derived from their
fears that Japan might perhaps be turned into a colony by
the white man. Commercial and industrial power was, in
their view, military power in embryo, a power for defending
the country: so they saw nothing wrong in creating political
parties which represented the interests of commerce and
industry.

The soldiers and the right-wing of the Shōwa period lost
sight of this crucial point. Consider the Pacific War. If Itō
Hirobumi (d. 1909) and his fellow-statesmen had been involved, they would first have made a comparison of commercial and industrial strengths and secondly looked at the
weapons they already possessed. But the soldiers of the

Shōwa period had been brought up in a mood of security after the Russo-Japanese War. They had an agrarian way of thinking, and were inclined to assess military strength by the possession of weapons. To give serious consideration to commerce and industry seems to have been anathema to them. An anti-commercial spirit was already abroad.

If they had had a genuine feeling of crisis—like the feeling prevalent among those elder Meiji statesmen—that Japan might perhaps be defeated, they would have persuaded the *zaibatsu* to go out to Manchuria and commercialise and industrialise it as rapidly as possible. Manchukuo was founded on a feeling of security: 'the land of the gods cannot be defeated'. Anti-commercial feelings took priority over the creation of a force to defend the country.

Had the political parties with a base in commerce and industry been healthy and sound, there is no doubt that we would never have gone to war. It is well-known that the *zaibatsu* disliked the idea of going to war with Great Britain and the United States.

Defeat brought to Japan once more the atmosphere of an equestrian society. The whole world was astounded by the development of commerce and industry in Japan at the time of the Meiji Restoration because the belief was prevalent among white men at that time that the coloured races could not create modern industries. The speed of development and the revival of commerce and industry after the war was both admired and feared. However, in these pages, we have glanced over several centuries of Japanese history, have seen a pattern emerging in which, every 40 years, an anti-commercial spirit suddenly blazes forth. Forty years have already passed since the defeat and I feel uneasy about certain symptoms which are gradually making themselves felt. The government is too ready to raise the tax on businesses, while protecting the agricultural community too much.

NOTES

1. The Kyoho reforms were a series of reforms and retrenchments carried out by the Tokugawa Shogunate during the Kyōhō era (1716–35) and the following decade under the direction of the Eighth Shogun Yoshimune Tokugawa.
2. The Kansei reforms (1789–93) were the second of the three reforms of the Tokugawa Shogunate.
3. The Tenpo reforms of 1841–43 were the last of the reforms of the Tokugawa Shogunate.
4. Manabe was originally an actor, a profession which was not, in the common acceptance of that time, highly regarded and a class decidedly inferior to that of a samurai. Arai Hakuseki was a profound scholar, unrivalled in his day, but he twice switched his feudal allegiance and took service under a third house.

    Yet the policy of Manabe and Hakuseki was, by and large, it must be admitted, a good one. In fact, people who might be termed extravagant in the Genroku era, the Fifth Shogun's era, considered an age of pomp and luxury, would have been thought to be enjoying an ordinary standard of living under the Sixth and Seventh Shoguns during Manabe's and Hakuseki's administration.
5. Cf. Takekoshi Yosaburō, Nihon *Keizai-shi* (History of the Japanese Economy) 1929, vol. 4, pp. 197–8.
6. On Tanuma, cf. my book *Fuhai no jidai* (An age of corruption), Bungei Shunju, 1975.

14 The World Turns Towards an Agrarian Ideology

WE CANNOT DISCUSS PROGRESSIVE OR REACTIONARY ATTITUDES IN TERMS OF DIFFERENCES IN THE FORMS OF SOCIETY

My first premise was that an agrarian society is one in which a feeling of security is characterised by the very roots of existence, and that an equestrian society is one based on ability. And I have interpreted Japan as an agrarian society, and the Mongolia of Genghis Khan, and America after its advance into the West, as equestrian societies.

I think this contrast is useful in understanding both Japan and America. However, having taken the contrast this far, I think I may have given the impression that in contrast to the agrarian society in which 'harmony' is the highest value, in which ability is envied, and where an air of stupidity prevails, the equestrian society, centred on ability and justice, has advanced further and is more gallant and dashing.

This, in fact, has, I think, been the general opinion until now. The Meiji Restoration strove to outstrip and to overtake Europe and America as highly developed nations; and post-war Japan, prostrate in defeat, strove to overtake America. Great Britain or the United States are, in one case or the other, the exemplars. When differences emerged between American and Japanese ways of doing things, those differences were interpreted as 'Japanese backwardness'. Has not the time come, however, for us to understand that it is rather unusual in the history of mankind to view the differences in the forms which societies adopt as differences between the advanced on the one hand and the primitive or backward on the other? If we take ancient China as an agrarian society, the northern people

174

called Pei Ti (Northern Barbarians) were an equestrian people, often victorious in battle. Just as the Mongols of the Yuan dynasty conquered the whole of China, so did the Ch'ing of Manchuria, although far inferior numerically to the Chinese. Yet it never remotely occurred to the Chinese to think that their culture was inferior to that of their conquerors. In fact, culturally speaking, the conquerors were overcome by the conquered.

The same can be said of Europe. Europe was frequently invaded and conquered by purely equestrian peoples, but even though they were over-run, they did not think their culture was inferior. They thought, simply, 'We're different; that's all'.

WHAT EXPLAINS THE VICTORY OF THE CIVILISATION OF MODERN WESTERN EUROPE?

The various conquests by Europeans and Americans in modern times, however, are of quite another kind. Not only was a difference felt between the culture of the conqueror and that of the conquered, but the culture of the conquered was held to be inferior. Europe and the United States constituted a society which had technology at its disposal, had rapidly mastered the natural sciences, and was not only strong in war but also felt itself superior in culture and civilisation.

The ancestors of the Indo-Germanic people sometimes referred to as Indo-Europeans, Aryans or 'white men', were originally chiefly engaged in agriculture and were raisers of livestock on a small scale. However, as their population increased and their cultural standards rose, commerce developed in the same way as it did in Japan.

Christian missionaries' reports indicated that the Sakai-Osaka region of the Azuchi Momoyama period (of the 16th century) could be likened to the London of Elizabeth I. Sakai was also compared with Venice which at that time was a commercial centre of the same standing as London.

In a warrior-society of the agrarian-type, like that of Japan, where anti-commercial sentiments were strong, trade could only be carried on in a form from which the vitality had been drained. From Europe, on the other hand, fleets were discovering new continents, and industry followed suit. The characteristic feature of modern Europe and the United States is the extensive development of commerce and industry on an originally agrarian basis. The development of Japanese and European ability in the fields of science and mathematics were parallel at this time, which can be seen from the commentaries on the era; it was even suggested that Seki Takakazu (d. 1708) discovered the differential calculus and the integral calculus several years before Leibniz and Newton. But in the Edo of the Genroku period there were no outlets for technology. There was no call for weaponry or guns in an agrarian society whose sole objective was to preserve peace and harmony.

That a man like Hiraga Gennai (d. 1779) should have been born in Japan in the Edo period was a tragedy. Gennai showed imaginative talent from a young age, and he left his position as head of a low ranking samurai. He went to Edo and pursued the study of herbal medicine, later on initiating a symposium of naturalists which presented some 1300 animal, plant and mineral specimens. In 1763 he published his *Classification of Various Materials*, considered his magnum opus. Later on he produced satirical novels and Edo comic literature, known as 'Kokkeibon'. He also experimented making asbestos cloth, thermometers, Dutch-style pottery and conducted surveys for ore deposits. He tried his hand at wool manufacturing, and produced several texts for puppet plays called Joruri. However, at a time of disappointments with his mining ventures he became increasingly aware that the rank-conscious society of his time was too rigid to recognise his individuality and special genius. Even his successful experiments with electricity offered him no consolation and in 1779, in a fit of madness, he killed one of his disciples and died the following year in prison. Commerce and craftsmanship spread freely in Western Europe and the kind of gifts he had would have been highly and widely prized there. The pioneers of the natural sciences in Europe encountered resistance and persecution from the churches and the forces of conservatism in Europe, but nonetheless they were far freer than they would have been in Japan.

Above all, the fact that such a place as America existed was conducive to the flowering of talent as well as to the encouragement of commerce and industry. In the new continent, the application of talent and invention to commerce and industry was considered to be normal and productive. It was very different for the Japanese who had no means of escaping from the agrarian shogunate which never ceased to issue prohibitions hostile to talent and proclaimed 'You must never invent anything new'.[1]

To put matters simply, Japan, until the Azuchi-Momoyama period, created a culture roughly comparable to that of Western Europe, but after that period she 'closed the country' and became locked in her own agrarian forms. So, whereas in Japan commerce and industry turned into something like potted *bonsai*, Western Europe built on its agrarian foundations and commerce and industry spread their branches like enormous trees. Hence when white men came to Japan, there was not only a difference in the forms of culture, there was a difference between superior and inferior.

THE 21ST CENTURY, 'JAPAN'S CENTURY': THE BASIS OF THIS EXPECTATION

What will happen to Japan from now on? If the occasion presents itself, if today's peace collapses, and an equestrian society emerges, Japan might adopt the ability principle. Great changes would occur in society, men like Hideyoshi and Ito Hirobumi would emerge; but as history has shown us, sooner or later we would revert to an agrarian society once peace and security were again achieved. Of course, if a great nuclear war broke out that would be the end of the planet itself, but that lies beyond the scope of our reflections. I am no Herman Kahn, but I think that if peace continues between the United States and the Soviet Union, and the world moves within the framework of a tolerable peace, there is a strong possibility that the 21st century will be Japan's century. Pre-war Japan was destined to fail because the agrarian ideology, in which army and bureaucracy felt secure, put pressure on commerce and industry. Success was achieved in the post-war period because the agrarian principle worked within a framework of commerce and industry.

Fear of bankruptcy is the great motivator of commercial and industrial enterprises. That is the equestrian ideology at work. But their employees, from top to bottom, work in accordance with agrarian concepts, and inside the enterprise it is not easy for competition to exist. Once harmony is easily maintained, the enterprise becomes a village, a body with a collective destiny. An enterprise had, in most cases, its own trade union. We may say that the strength of Japanese enterprises today lies in a fortuitous historical situation in which enterprises with an equestrian ideology, in which ability is paramount, have as their principle of internal control not equestrian leadership but agrarian harmony.

Mr Iida Tsuneo has defined the main features of Japanese companies—and Japanese society itself—as 'the place where the ordinary man works well'. There are only two conditions in which the ordinary man works well. One is a society with a confident leadership of the equestrian style which can ensure that its orders are obeyed, like the United States and Europe in the past; or, alternatively, as in a Japanese village, a society in which men have a job they consider worthwhile. It is no doubt essential that in the latter type of society the ordinary man should not be tormented by feelings of frustration or by the profitless spirit of envy. In that case, it is vital for those at the top to base themselves firmly on the rule of morality and aim at spiritual cultivation. Character is what counts.

Let me adduce here an example of an enterprise in which vastly different results have been achieved through eliminating futile envy from among the ordinary working men (the story is told by Mr Hasegawa Keitarō). Nissan (Datsun) is a world-class enterprise, representative of Japan at its best, hence its employees have no anxieties about whether or not their company will collapse. There is a feeling of security from which we should assume that an agrarian concept is at work. They have, though, a system of inviting suggestions from employees in the various unit factories. This suggestion system constitutes, precisely, an ability element. Now no one thinks there is any difference in the quality of employees in one Nissan factory as against another, so you would expect that the number of suggestions per man, in any one factory, would be roughly the same. Yet there are considerable discrepancies. In the Zama factory, there were 17 items per man per year; in the other factories only eight. Why this discrepancy? Does it spring from differences in the system of salaries and rewards offered for the suggestions?

Surprisingly, in the Zama factory, in contrast with the other factories, there is no production incentive bonus to encourage a spirit of competition among the employees. There is simply a monthly salary system. When managers on study tours from automobile factories in Europe and the US observe this, they openly express their incredulity.

Furthermore, the reward money for suggestions in the Zama factory reached ¥140 million in 1979. But here, too, there is a difference from the other factories: individual suggestions rapidly decreased, and in recent years they have been put forward by departments and groups only. In one department, bonus money of ¥2 400 000 was earned which provided free trips for the whole department. Bonus money for suggestions in Europe or the United States would naturally be earned by an individual. These are facts which foreigners (people from an equestrian society) cannot easily understand.

So a paradoxical situation has arisen in which the enthusiasm for making suggestions has increased in direct proportion to the absence of obvious incentives. It shows how much the ordinary man in an agrarian system dislikes his ability being evaluated. It is unpleasant for him to be associated with differentiation even in the number of suggestions put forward. However, as long as the suggestion is not one which singles you out, you can happily make suggestions on behalf of the company, because the company—just like the village—is the fundamental basis of your life.

While the outer framework we call the company functions according to a commercial and industrial equestrian principle, internal harmony is preserved at its core to a degree we can identify as agrarian, and production will increase.

This can be done in Japan. What would happen if it were tried abroad?

As the present world trend is turning against leadership of the equestrian type, does not the Japanese type inevitably offer a pointer to the future?

A WORLD SITUATION IN WHICH THE AGRARIAN TYPE OFFERS ADVANTAGES EVEN IN THE DEVELOPMENT OF ULTRA-MODERN TECHNOLOGY

So the point, I feel, is this: we have possibly reached a stage in which Japan's methods today offer advantages not only in the manufacture of industrial products, but even in the development of ultra-modern technology.

For instance, any advanced country recognises the importance of the development of ultra LSI (Large-scale integrated circuits) in future production. In Japan, an ultra LSI research cooperation group centred on the Ministry of International Trade and Industry was set up in 1976 and a large research project was announced with ¥30 billion from the government and ¥40 billion from private sources, a total of ¥70 billion (approximately £30 million).

The private sector consisted of five major computer companies, Fujitsū, Hitachi, and others. To further this project, the research co-operation group was to obtain the advice of Dr Reona Ezaki, a Nobel Prize winner for his studies in semi-conductors. It was rumoured, however, that Dr Ezaki was less than keen about the idea of this research co-operation group. His response was doubtful: the prospects of success through a research association of several companies were almost nil, in anything as advanced as ultra LSI research.

Perhaps he had American companies in mind. In the event, the project was brought to a triumphant conclusion in March 1980. The measure of its achievement lies in the very fact that IBM exerted strong pressure for the results to be put in the public domain. The quality of co-operation among the Japanese enterprises was high, far exceeding what Dr Ezaki had supposed possible.

If colleagues from different Japanese enterprises can co-operate so successfully, it can easily be imagined that the level of co-operation will be even higher within the same enterprise. In village society there has always been a communal co-operation on such burning questions as when to plant rice or when to harvest because in the Japanese climate one day's hesitation could spoil the year's harvest.

Perhaps in today's advanced scientific technology, since all specialisations have become ultra-particularised, then everybody in the team plodding along in concert with everybody else step by step—the type of agrarian co-operation—offers more advantages than the methods of the lone wolf researcher. I was amazed to notice, in reading a book by Mr Moritani Masanori (a senior specialist on comparative technologies for the Nomura Research Institute) called, *Japan's Technological Power (Nihon no gijutsuryoku)*,[2] what a wealth of concrete instances he could bring forward to show the debt owed by Japan's technological power to the Japanese way of life. What Mr Moritani calls 'Japanese' corresponds roughly to what I have called in this book 'agrarian ideology'.

NOTES

1.   One of the anti-merchant decrees issued during the Kansei Reforms (1789–93) stipulated that you must not invent anything new.
2.   NonBooks, Shodensha, 1980.

15 Conclusion

In concluding this book it may be of some interest to venture a few conjectures concerning the future of the Japanese people from the viewpoint of the agrarian-equestrian dichotomy.

As of 1988 Japanese society is, in comparison with other advanced industrialised nations, functioning very well, with high-tech products selling briskly at home and abroad, with foreign exchange reserve accumulating steadily, with dwindling crime and divorce rates and the unemployment rate constantly kept to a low level. A number of reasons could be proposed which explain this prosperous status quo. Ours is only one of them, but will shed much light on an important but less known aspect of Japanese business organisations or corporations.

In pre-war Japan (roughly until 1945) most Japanese corporations were managed, very much like those in other industrial nations, on classical capitalistic principles. The owners and managers of corporations felt quite free to fire their employees in hard times. Wages and salaries were generally based more on the merits and efficiency of employees than on any seniority system. In other words, Japanese corporations with the exception of a few companies, such as the Matsushita Electric Company, used to be like their counterparts in America or Europe. A corporation based on the principle of ability may collapse at any time if its leader is not good enough. In this sense corporations based on the capitalistic principles are to be called of 'equestrian' nature in our terminology.

After the end of the war in 1945 a fundamental change took place in the nature of Japanese corporations. Seen from the outside, Japanese corporations functioned just as in the pre-war days. They collapsed at any time when their leaders were not competent enough and were defeated in competition. The governing principle within the Japanese companies, however, underwent a far-reaching change. It has become virtually impossible to fire employees, even in hard times when business is lagging. Without conscious

182

planning by any particular body, the Japanese styled life-employment system has taken deep root. Though one tends to regard this system as characteristic of traditional Japanese society, it is, in fact, of recent post-war origin.

The atmosphere in a typical Japanese corporation is observed to be similar to that in the traditional agrarian village. All employees feel more or less safe in their 'village'. Most employees feel happy to be with their co-workers. Comparatively few workers have private extra-corporational activities. Their corporations are the village they belong to. In one word, their corporations are possessed of communal and 'agrarian' atmosphere and features.

However communal and congenial they feel about their corporational 'villages', corporations are corporations; they may collapse at any time due to hard times or inefficient management. Thus, post-war Japanese corporations are of 'equestrian' nature as far as their framework is concerned, while 'agrarian' insofar as their inner governing principle is concerned. The present Japanese corporations are, in a sense, behaving exactly in the manner of profit-seeking ability-based groups ('mounted bandits'), yet component members are far more like peasants in agrarian villages.

This combination of two contrasting principles in typical Japanese corporations has proven effective in most fields of post-war industry and commerce. The 'villagers' of a corporation co-operate for the prosperity of their 'village' in a more or less self-effacing manner just as landed peasants used to do for their village. This self-effacing element in their activity has turned out to be advantageous for the technical developments, which require real co-operation among engineers and workers, and for the worldwide activities of gigantic trading firms. Japanese co-operations are generous about investing large sums for the education of their members, because they know such investments are rewarded amply by the elevated quality of their employees. In many countries corporations hesitate to sink money into the education of their employees, who, if better educated, would not hesitate to find better-paid jobs from other corporations.

Will this happy combination of two principles, equestrian and agrarian, continue to be a lasting feature of Japanese corporations? It may well last for quite a long time, but it is also a fact that more and more emphasis will be placed on personal merits than on seniority. In other words, it is quite probably that Japanese corporations will become more and more like those of other countries, while it is also possible that at the same time corporations of other nations will become more and more similar to those in Japan. Furthermore, feminist movements will surely militate against the continuance of combined agrarian and equestrian principles, being in the industrial world a movement of the equestrian principle *par excellence*. Women advocating feminist principles wish to see promotion based on merit, whereas promotion and salary increase are not based on these principles in Japanese corporational villages. Generally speaking, a mediocre, white-collar clerk of 45 years of age will receive far more than a brillinat white-collar worker of 30 years of age in the same corporation, the reason being that the 'elders' of the corporational villages take into consideration the familial conditions of their villagers as well as their merits. A man of 45 years of age may have children attending college, be paying back loans for his home, and, irrespective of his merits, he is in need of more income than a man of 30 years of age. This is commonly recognised in the Japanese corporational village. With the introduction of views such as those held by feminist thinkers into the 'village', the position and salary of each 'villager' will have to be decided purely on meritocratic principles, with the result that the spirit of the Japanese corporational village will pass away, and Japanese corporations will be managed in clearer accordance with capitalistic principles. Up to the present time the position of Japanese women in the business world is markedly different from that in our industrial nations. Whether Japan will follow their pattern or work out a new type of combined equestrian and agrarian principle remains to be seen.

Appendix

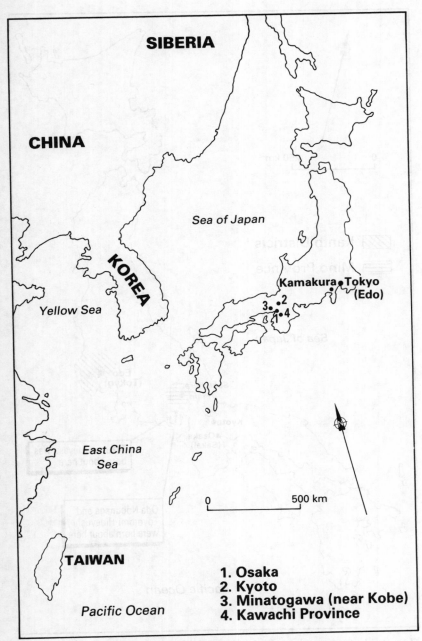

1. Osaka
2. Kyoto
3. Minatogawa (near Kobe)
4. Kawachi Province

MAP 1 *The Battle of Minatogawa, July 1336*

188

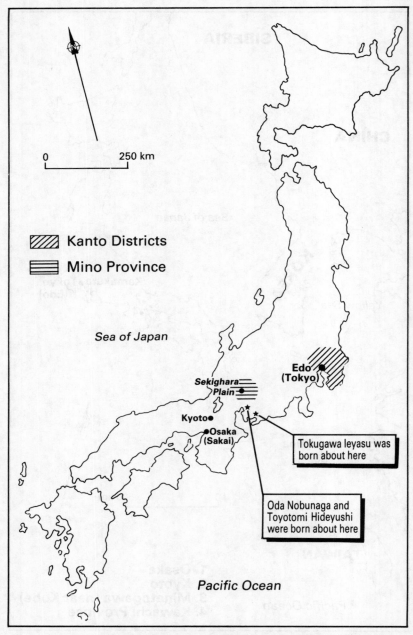

Kanto Districts

Mino Province

Sea of Japan

Edo
(Tokyo)

*Sekighara
Plain*

Kyoto●

●Osaka
(Sakai)

Tokugawa Ieyasu was
born about here

Oda Nobunaga and
Toyotomi Hideyushi
were born about here

Pacific Ocean

MAP 2   *Important places in Japan in the latter part of the 16th century,
which preceded the foundation of the Tokugawa Shogunate.*

189

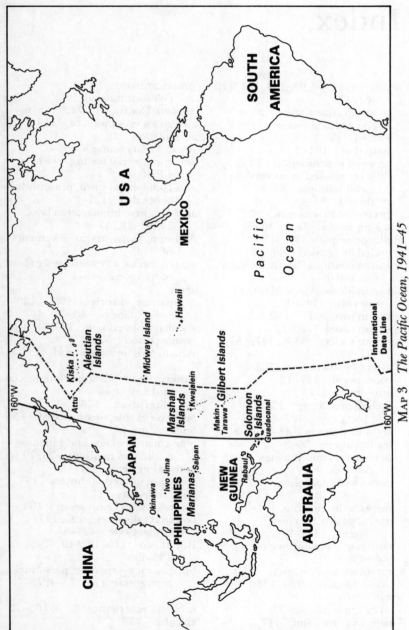

MAP 3   *The Pacific Ocean, 1941–45*

Index

Index 195